The Unruly Past

Laura Kalpakian

PAINT CREEK

Paint Creek Press
P.O. Box 964
Chippewa Falls, WI 54719
paintcreekpress.com
info@paintcreekpress.com

ISBN: 978-0-9972102-7-9

**Portions of some of these memoirs
appeared in different forms in:**

Homeground (Blue Heron Publishing
and Before Columbus Foundation, 1994)
The Confidence Woman (Longstreet Press, 1990)
*John Steinbeck: Centennial Reflections by
American Writers* (San Jose State Press, 2002)
Stone Stories Chapbook published by Armenian
International Women's Association, 1994
Victoria Magazine
Ararat Magazine

Pictured on front cover:
Haroutune Kalpakian age 5, 1891
Will Johnson age 12, 1899

This book is memoir. It reflects the author's
present recollections of experiences over time.

The novelist is one on whom nothing is lost.
~Henry James
"The Art of Fiction" 1888

DEDICATION

Pour toute la famille
Pour ceux qui sont tout près et ceux qui sont loin
Pour les vivants et les morts.
Ceux qu'on a perdus et retrouvés
Ceux qui ne sont pas encore nés.

ALSO BY LAURA KALPAKIAN

MEMORY INTO MEMOIR

THE GREAT PRETENDERS

THREE STRANGE ANGELS

THE MUSIC ROOM

A CHRISTMAS CORDIAL AND OTHER STORIES

AMERICAN COOKERY

THE MEMOIR CLUB

EDUCATING WAVERLEY

THE DELINQUENT VIRGIN

STEPS AND EXES

CAVEAT

GRACED LAND

COSETTE: A SEQUEL TO LES MISÉRABLES

FAIR AUGUSTO AND OTHER STORIES

CRESCENDO

THESE LATTER DAYS

BEGGARS AND CHOOSERS

A NOTE TO THE READER

Both sides of my family tend to recycle names. When my Armenian grandparents came to America they kept their last name, but changed their first names to Harry and Helen. Most of the other relatives changed everything. I have used the family's Armenian names for as long as they used them, then changing to the American names. Though my great-uncle Haigauz changed his name to Harry Clark, I have continued to refer to him as Haigauz to avoid confusion (and because we always called him Haigauz). The Armenian language has its own alphabet, and so all the names given here are offered phonetically, the best I can do. Some Armenian words are peculiar to my family and may reflect pronunciation or regionalisms from southeastern Turkey where they originated. We used the word *paklava* to describe what is generally known as *baklava*. Grape leaves rolled around a meat and rice mixture is generally known as *dolma*, or *sarma*. In my family we called it *derev*, which I have recently learned is the Armenian word for leaf.

Mormon family names appear often in different generations, though nearby one another in time. Thus, there is an Elaine Johnson (born 1915) my father's aunt, and there is an Elaine Johnson (b. 1922) my father's sister. I have tried to distinguish between William A. Johnson Senior (b. 1863) and William A. Johnson Junior (b. 1887) by referring to the latter (my grandfather) as Will. Fortunately, the two sisters who matter most to this chronicle, Lila and Anetta, their names do not duplicate. And yes, Anetta's name on all family documents has only one "n."

The Unruly Glossary at the back of this book offers further familial clarity to the interested reader. I should also add that some of the names in this book have been changed.

CONTENTS

1. THE NIGHT TRAIN TO FRANKFURT............................3

2. DECLARATIONS AND DENIALS 19

3. "BRIDE OF THE WAVES".................................77

4. THE UNBELIEVERS....................................... 131

5. WHY I DON'T WRITE FOR THE NEW YORK TIMES 167

6. THE WAYWARD APPRENTICE 195

7. REVEL AND PRESERVE................................ 237

8. "INCHBESSESS" 251

9. OF BOOKS AND BOYS.................................... 261

10. ANOTHER STORY.. 267

11. ACKNOWLEGMENTS....................................... 273

12. AN UNRULY GUIDE FOR READERS.......................... 275

13. ABOUT THE AUTHOR 281

The
Unruly
Past

Laura Kalpakian

THE NIGHT TRAIN TO FRANKFURT

Both of my grandfathers were born in 1887. William Andrew Johnson, Jr., my father's father, was born to devoutly Mormon parents in Idaho Territory in a shelter dug out from the earth, the "roof" supported by hand-hewn timbers. Eventually Will Johnson's father built the first brick house in Madison County, but not before four more children were born in the dugout which they then used for a chicken coop. Haroutune Kalpakian, my mother's father, was born to a wealthy mercantile Armenian family in Caesarea, Turkey. They moved in 1896 to Mersin, a polyglot seaport on the Eastern Mediterranean, why I do not know. At the start of the Armenian Genocide in 1915, the Turks arrested and imprisoned a family member in the city of Adana some miles inland. The Kalpakians left Mersin to go to his aid, and after many anguished months, he was freed on the very day he was to be hanged. The Kalpakians did not return to Mersin, where, so I understand, the Turks had confiscated their house. The family remained in Adana, and here my grandfather met my grandmother, and they married in the fall of 1917. They stayed in Adana until 1921when they were forced with bayonets on to trains going to Syria. The improbable convergence of these two families, two cultures—frontier Mormon pioneers, and urbanite Armenians in Turkey—was effected along the major fault lines of twentieth century history. The international and ethnic upheavals of World War I brought my mother's people to Los Angeles in 1923. After Pearl Harbor in December 1941, my father joined the Marine Reserves, and World War II propelled him out of the Mormon enclaves he had always known.

How to reconcile such divergent experience when it converges in one life, one's DNA? I sometimes felt—feel—myself to be a sort of rickety bridge perilously thrown across the chasm between these dual identities. Friends, editors, agents have, for years, urged me to write a memoir (especially since the memoir is one of my favorite genres) and I tried. I tried more than once. But I found that the two sides of my family simply would not be reconciled to the same page. And indeed, *The Unruly Past* proves this is still true. These dual identities remain for me, in some ways, still undefined. I do not have the Armenian language that would allow me to plunge deeply into my relatives' experience. Until it was too late, I didn't even know what questions to ask. When, as a child, I went to Armenian picnics with Grandma, my cheeks pinched by old folks chattering in Armenian and taught to say *Inchbessus*, I knew I was not like them. As for the Mormons, even as a child when we went to visit Utah and Idaho, I knew I was not like them, bland, and fair-haired with flat voices. In short, I knew who

I wasn't. I grew up on a sort of ethnic frontier, an undefined edge, constantly fraying. This is an uneasy place to live, but it is fruitful ground for a fiction writer.

In my past attempts at memoir, the Mormons and Armenians have refused to unite in narrative, and yet, ironically as ethnic and historical entities they share many canopy similarities. Both are tribes with strong religious and familial bonds. They are insular. Each has a specific word to describe anyone from outside the tribe, anyone Not One of Us. For the Armenians, the word is *odar* (spoken usually with a slight, dismissive shrug). The Saints, since their earliest beginnings, describe non-Mormons as Gentiles, the very term suggesting Old Testament conflicts facing the chosen people.

The Mormons and Armenians revere their respective pasts, histories full of persecution. Two thousand years ago the Armenians were the first Christian nation, a culture with their own art, literature, music, and architecture. They were conquered in the sixteenth century, and ever since endured endless assaults, particularly under the Ottoman Empire. The all too apt phrase "Starving Armenians" clung to them for the past one hundred years. The Mormons, from their earliest beginnings, suffered bloody persecutions as the Gentiles wrought violence on their settlements, forcing them ever further westward across America.

The Saints and Armenians also share a deep affiliation to a geographical region. For the Mormons, Utah. For the

Armenians the land of Mount Ararat, atop which, according to the Bible, Noah's ark once rested. Though the 1919 peace treaties after World War I gave the Armenians their historic homeland, this fledgling country was quickly swallowed by the Soviet Union, and became one of the Soviet Socialist Republics. Not until 1990 and the fall of the Soviet Union did Armenia become its own country. Ironically though, for two such peoples committed to sacred geographically-known places, both are also represented by vast diasporas. Mormons, though a thoroughly American religion, are an international faith. Even in their earliest days, before 1850, they proselytized abroad, especially in Scandinavia and Northern Europe. Now the Church of Jesus Christ of Latter-day Saints has temples and churches, schools and universities all over the world. The Armenian diaspora was created over centuries; tight-knit Armenian communities hunkered down, often in hostile circumstances. In the 1920s after the Armenian Genocide they established or expanded international communities, especially in the Middle East, places like Egypt and Syria and Jerusalem. More recently, since 1990, and the fall of the Soviet Union, influxes of international Armenians have come together in Southern California; they are all Armenian, but they carry the cultures of distant destinations. They do not always see eye to eye.

To cross the frontier in this, the European sense of that term suggests, as my high school French teacher, Madame Bateen, made plain, a confrontation with *history*, with language and identity: one shows one's papers, declares one's origins, crosses into another country, becoming foreign (and later, for the Kalpakians, becoming Americans, naturalized citizens). But there's another sense of frontier, the American understanding of the term, and this is how my father's people lived it. They crossed vast expanses, hunkered down briefly in settlements, and left, moving restlessly along the Idaho/Utah corridor, To cross the frontier in this, the American context, suggests a confrontation with *nature*, venturing into unknowable dangers, unmapped places: one becomes a pioneer.

In any event—pioneer or immigrant—contented people do not uproot, repudiate their pasts and move on. To leave one's home (or homeland) requires energy, strength, determination, or perhaps mere physical stamina and simple desperation. Somewhere in the past of most American families, such restless people exist. Whether emigrants from abroad, or westering wagon trains or people leaving the rural south and moving to new lives in the cities of the north and west, in their hearts and minds these discontented people carry their memories and music, their old recipes, for some their old languages. In short, they bear with them identities that cannot be declared at Customs, nor sloughed off from overburdened Conestogas rumbling west, nor dropped off the back of a lumbering truck. Their remembered identities and adventures are gradually converted into family lore that refines difficult, even painful experience into the well-made, oft-told tale. These narratives become anecdotal inheritance passed down to the generations that follow. They serve to tame the unruly past, though they do not make it docile by any means. Collectively these stories preserve family identity; over time they evolve into truth, or at the very least, they are believed—however diminished the nugget of reality at the center of that story, however fanciful the embellishments around that nugget. On the Kalpakian side of my family their stories were eventually whittled down to three oft-told tales that had been purged of pain. On the Johnson side, their stories were expanded to strain credulity and reward righteousness. The truth or falsity of these stories, in my opinion, matters little. As a writer, I am more interested in what is left out.

I can write this book because in 1944 Bill Johnson was serving as a pharmacist's mate in the Navy, stationed on an aircraft carrier in Long Beach, slated to ship out to the Pacific. Peggy Kalpakian, daughter of a Los Angeles grocer, was a business administration major at the University of Southern California. These two young people met at a USO dance, and six months later they were married by a navy chaplain. When the War ended, my dad got a Masters in Public Health from Cal Berkeley, and for a time worked for the Red Cross. After that he worked as a pharmaceutical rep in Southern California while my mother stayed home with their four children, two sons, two daughters, of whom I am the eldest. In 1951 they bought a tract house in Reseda, in the San Fernando Valley. For the seven years we lived there we shared holidays and Sunday lunches with my Armenian grandparents at their house on Olympic Boulevard in Los Angeles, along with my mother's three sisters, Angagh, Betty and Harriett, their husbands, and children.

Before 1956 we seldom saw any of the extended Johnson family who lived in Utah and Idaho. After 1956 we visited them every summer for at least a decade. My mother, though she never expressly said as much, was, I believe, wary of the Johnsons' tribalism. Her own family ties were local, all on her mother's side, and limited to a couple of aunts, a few uncles, and a mere four cousins. The Johnsons, on the other hand, were a vast, restless clan; my father had forty-odd first cousins. My mother, too, probably winced at the Johnsons' generally easygoing grammar. Their sometimes raucous humor was at odds with the understated decorum, the attention to manners that she grew up with in a family still learning to be American. On our summertime treks to Utah and Idaho, some of the Johnsons were not always warm or welcoming to my mother. They viewed her as urban, foreign (she was born in Constantinople) even, in the parlance of the day, "alien." I do not remember any active unkindness visited on us, but a ripple of distrust informed both sides. My father was probably unaware of the undercurrent. Undercurrents were not his forte.

Will and Mae Johnson, my father's parents only once came to visit us in Reseda, in 1953 when I would have been about eight. (They were always called Grandma Johnson or Grandpa Johnson, whereas the Armenians were just Grandma and Grandpa.) We took Will and Mae into LA for a Sunday lunch at my grandparents' house, not a big gathering, just us, and my youngest aunt who still lived at home. My grandmother would have been cooking all morning, and probably the whole day before, making *derev*, rolling up a meat and rice mixture in brined grape leaves, and baking it in a sauce. She would have carefully, continually checked the oven to be certain the *lamajunes* did not overbake. She would have made the *paklava* by hand. She would have made the pilaf at the last minute. (Food was the only part of their past the Kalpakians did not slough off in their haste to assimilate.) When it was time to eat we gathered at their huge dining room table, my grandfather at the head. We all said the Lord's Prayer. He raised his wineglass and said, as he always did in still-accented English, "Welcome to our house."

Will and Mae, devout Mormons, did not drink wine or coffee or tea. The food went round the table. Will and Mae nibbled gingerly, even suspiciously. After a while Mae turned to my dad, and said, "Well, Bill, I guess you've grown to like this stuff."

I don't remember what he replied, or if my mother stifled a grin or a grimace, but in retrospect this cracks me up because it was true. He had grown to like this stuff! In nine years of marriage, Bill had come to pride himself on barbequing shish kebab. He loved my grandmother's sticky-sweet *paklava*! He loved my mom's *lamajune*, rice pilaf and her stuffed zucchinis! He loved my grandfather's old country folk tales, the Hodja stories! In fact, he loved Harry and Helen Kalpakian! Assimilation can work both ways, Mae! Harry and Helen Kalpakian had become Americans, and Bill Johnson had become as Armenian as it is possible for any ex-Mormon to be.

Yvette Bateen probably never thought she would end up teaching French to a bunch of teenage louts in a desert-burg like San Bernardino, California. She had graduated from the University of Clermont-Ferrand. I know this from my high school yearbook. Clermont-Ferrand is in the Auvergne, a region forever darkened with the shadow of the Vichy government under the Nazi Occupation. In those heady months following the June 1944 Normandy landings, the Americans marching through France were seen as heroes, liberators, and more than one French girl fell in love with a handsome Yank. Yvette Bateen married hers. I am speculating here, but how else would someone so unique, sophisticated and exotic ever have fetched up as a teacher at San Bernardino High School?

Perhaps Yvette Bateen went into teaching because it gave her to the opportunity to speak nonstop French. She allowed no English to be spoken in her classroom. We did not learn from lisping "This is the pen of my aunt." Madame Bateen snorted at such banality. Sure, she used a textbook, but she enlivened our vocabulary with *Paris Match*. (Recollection flickers over a memory that Madame Bateen took shit from the school because *Paris Match* included pictures of Brigitte Bardot and other St. Tropez scantily clad beauties, but she did not relent. Or she might have said she'd replace the magazines and then scoffed at such narrow-minded priggery. They stayed on the shelves.) We listened to Yves Montand and Edith Piaf while we wrote up our exercises. Her teaching included long tirades in her native language about how everything was better in France. In correcting our ignorance of French culture, she reminded us daily, she was doing us an enormous favor. Her passion for her native country, its culture and history was equal only to her contempt for her students.

She had wild, dyed hair and wore cats'-eye glasses, brilliant red lipstick, and high-heeled sandals with bare legs. She was unabashedly female. This isn't to say she was beautiful. She wasn't. But she did not camouflage the fact that she was a woman. The other female teachers, young or old, they dressed and moved like sawhorses with breasts. Madame Bateen was undeniably sexy, cold, crisp, and flamboyant. She would slip out and have a cigarette at the back of the bungalow between classes and never seemed to think that we should wink at her transgression. She cared nothing for what we thought. She regarded us with the disdain that only the French can muster.

One particular afternoon—so hot and breeze-less even the flies were comatose—she was waxing on about the frontier, about crossing the frontier. We had no idea what she was talking about, and our blank stares conveyed as much. "Le frontier! Le frontier!" She shouted, growing more animated.

One of the boys started singing "Davy, Davy Crockett, King of the Wild Frontier."

"You sound like a donkey. Shut up," she said with no regard for his tender self-image. By now thoroughly exasperated, she spoke in English and described the frontier properly and according to the European understanding.

"Oh Madame Bateen, you mean a border!" Offered one student, "To cross the border!"

"No I do not mean a border," scoffed Madame Bateen, her sneer settling that kid's hash. "I mean one stops to cross the frontier when one goes into another country. One has one's papers checked at the frontier, n'est-ce-pas, one becomes foreign."

Madame Bateen taught me a great deal more than how to conjugate verbs. Her passion for her homeland contributed to my being a confirmed Francophile. When I first went to Europe in my twenties, I thought of her constantly as I used my schoolgirl French with abandon in Paris, Avignon, Nice, all over France, downright giddy to feel myself becoming more competent, perhaps, I dared to think, even more cosmopolitan.

Toward the end of the trip I parted with some friends in Nice and got on the night train to Frankfurt, Germany. From there I would change trains for Marburg, Germany where I had a grad school friend who had married a German. I had just come off the beach at Nice, and got to the station just in time to get on the train. I found a compartment, put my suitcase in the rack, and took a seat beside a plain, middle aged woman. She did not speak English, but no matter, thanks to Madame Bateen, I spoke French, *n'est-ce-pas?* She was on her way to an all-France Latter-day Saints conference in Grenoble.

"Mais oui," I said impulsively, "Je suis une Saint!"

She was delighted! Had I actually been to Salt Lake?

"Oui! La famille de mon pere habite tout à Utah!"

Had I been to the beautiful Salt Lake temple? Practiced baptism for the dead?

I instantly regretted having bounded into this conversation. My French was certainly not equal to nuance. I should not have said "Je suis une Saint!" I most emphatically was no longer une Saint, but I could not hope to clarify my complicated relationship with the church. I probably could not even do so in English, but all I could eke out in French was that my grandfather was "morte," but he had been "un grand Mormon et tres..." whatever was the word for devout, which she supplied.

However, having once declared myself to be any kind of Mormon at all, this woman was my Sister. She shared her lovely basket of food with me which I accepted with a guilty *merci mille fois*. She assured me she was happy to watch my things while I wandered the train (I was eager to escape her questions). She looked askance, worried for me when she got off the train that night, and it filled with what seemed like a whole regiment of French soldiers in uniform. Six or seven of them crammed into my compartment. With them, trust me, I did not use my schoolgirl French. I faked sleep.

I spent a sleepless, long night ride surrounded by snoring soldiers. At dawn the train stopped, I think in Strasbourg, and the soldiers got off. I changed trains there, going on to Frankfurt where I would change yet again for Marburg. On the train to Frankfurt, across from me sat an elderly couple, and beside me sat a tall, well-dressed man, older than I, but not unattractive. He and they conversed in a language I could not even place. I kept my silence and dozed until the train slowed when we crossed out of France, and I saw the sign: FRONTIER. As uniformed Germans customs men entered the train I longed to tell Madame Bateen that at last I understood! I could hear her crisp voice! *One crosses the frontier, one goes into another country. One has one's papers checked at the frontier, n'est-ce-pas, one becomes foreign.* And in becoming foreign I felt a flash of—not understanding or anything as complex as insight—but a wordless, fleeting flicker of phantom apprehension on behalf of my Armenian grandparents. Though at this time I knew almost nothing of their true experience, I felt the glint of dread they must surely have experienced as immigrants, to say nothing of refugees, to be at the mercy of uniformed foreign officials who could make any choices they liked about my grandparents' fate. For me the train suffused with both drama and menace (much of it also admittedly compounded from many movies) as the border guard dealt first with the tall man and the old couple, speaking in German which I did not understand, but they clearly did. Then the guard turned to me and spoke in a peremptory fashion, and again I did not understand.

"Your papers, Miss," said the tall man in English, "Your passport. They want to see your passport."

I had nothing to hide, but my heart was pounding as I fumbled into my bag, and gave the German guard my passport. He returned it to me, thanked us in a barking, bureaucratic fashion for our cooperation, and went into the next compartment. Soon the guards called out to one another; they got off, and the train moved.

I thanked the tall man in English and smiled at the old couple. They were Swedes, as it turned out, and didn't speak English, but the tall man did. He was American. He was a translator in the foreign language department at Cal Berkeley. Amazingly he was going on to Marburg to attend a Bach concert in a famous church. Oh, god! Was I not a truly a fortunate pilgrim? I had totally lucked out! I had been well fed by the kindly French Mormon matron. I wasn't raped by the French soldiers. And here was someone who spoke fluent German to translate for me in a place where all I could do was stammer and stupidly point. When in Frankfurt we changed trains for Marburg all I had to do was follow him! In fact, once in Marburg he graciously helped me find my girlfriend's house. He asked if I would like to go to the concert with him. I would.

This Nice-to-Frankfurt overnight ride was emblematic of my family past, even my very identity. A fiction writer is best served by not being too cozy or comfy or pillowed or safe, not sharing all the assumptions of one's companions, be they family or fellow travelers. To the Mormons I owed the happy warmth offered to me by the Saintly matron, though in truth I was a total imposter. To the Armenians I owed the sense of being foreign, being wary, observant and on edge, though I was in no particular danger. A fiction writer needs empathy, maybe even ungovernable empathy, the instinct, ability to offer tendrils of understanding, to expand on those tendrils, and yet, also, to keep sufficient distance. The fiction writer never quite declares oneself at the frontier; one's papers and passports are always suspect, and to some degree false, just by virtue of being a writer. The past is a foreign country, an unruly country. To explore it, one packs what one can for the journey, faces all sorts of frontiers fraught with both possibility and peril.

~June 2021

CHAPTER ONE

DECLARATIONS AND DENIALS

The water goes, the sand remains. The person dies, the memory remains.

~*Armenian proverb*

I

They are leaving. They stare out from the passport picture which is haphazardly glued to the nondescript little book with coarse pages. Passport and photo are both embossed with the star and crescent. On this date in 1923 they declare officially that they are Turkish subjects, though they are not Turkish. Turkey is their home, but not their country, the land where they have lived for generations, for as long as anyone can remember. They are lucky to have lived at all. Their ethnicity is nowhere stated; they are Armenians. Eight years before, in 1915, under the cover of war, the Turks systemically began decimating the Armenian minority living within their borders. The Turks marched more than a million Armenian men, women, children into desert exile, to death by starvation, or merely massacred them by various means not as quick and dignified as firing squads. Turkey is soon to be rid of a few more Armenians: the family of Haroutune Kalpakian, his wife, Haigouhi, a daughter and a baby, as well as Haigouhi's younger brother Haigauz, they are leaving. They have been spared death and exile, but they are fleeing nonetheless.

Clearly in this passport photo they do not want to look like refugees. Haroutune, the husband, wears a tie, a high collar, a vest. The passport describes him of medium size with a round face, clear eyes, regular nose, normal mouth, a thin moustache and no beard. His hair is visibly receding at thirty-six. His posture, the sharp angle of his right elbow, his direct gaze all create an effect of pomp, of dignity, not in keeping with the iron bars in the background behind the family. Officially, the passport declares him without *qualité ou profession*. The child, Angagh, four years old, looks skeptical. The baby, Pakradouhi, bundled up, asleep, no more than a round face atop a blanket and beneath a cap. The young wife, Haigouhi, twenty-two, her arms around the baby, looks stunned. Her eyes are not at all like her husband's. Her gaze goes behind the photographer, per-haps beyond him, through him. She seems to have seen everything and to see nothing. The iron bars behind them accentuate their differences of expression, and give a grim cast to this austere photo. The passport is stamped from the *4me Section* of the Constantinople police. It says so in French and Turkish.

They both speak French, but the commerce of their everyday lives in Constantinople, in any Turkish city, would have been conducted in Turkish. Armenian language was forbidden. Armenian language, religion, culture and identity—Christian in this Muslim country—had come to be a secret thing, confined to the home, to intimate discourse, familial exchange. It would not have been the language spoken here at the police station where stamps are affixed to their passport indicating that the fees have been paid. (There is nothing to indicate that the bribes have been paid, but they have.) The passport says their destination is *Amérique, Etats-Unis* and the point of their voyage, *chez ses parents*. In French *chez ses parents* signifies family, that is Haigouhi's family, her older brother, her older sister and brother-in-law. Haroutune's family? Well, they are dispersed forever. He will never see them again. One hundred years will pass before their descendants reconnect.

The passport, it is noted, is good for one year from today, 26 March 1923, the very day the sleeping baby, Pakradouhi, is one year old.

Did they celebrate her first birthday? From the *4me Section* of the police, the Kalpakians went home (according to this passport that only came into my hands after my grandmother's death in 1987) to the rue patchadji, No. 46, Constantinople. A noisy journey through a city still suffering, politically roiling in the wake of Turkey and Germany's 1918 defeat. The victorious Allies, the French and British, remain very much a presence here, even in 1923. The family's flat at No. 46 is three flights up. Two bedrooms and a kitchen. The latrine is shared, but there is no flush toilet. The kitchen has cold running water, but not hot. Haigouhi Kalpakian would have set out the little plates, enamel, blue on one side, white on the other, cooked the evening meal, probably bulgur wheat and onions, and closed the shutters against the evening air (she had a horror of drafts all her life) and against the cries at sunset, the haunting wails from the city's minarets calling the majority faithful to face East and pray to Allah.

Haroutune and Haigouhi Kalpakian were of the minority Christians, now even more of a minority since the Turks had annihilated half of the Armenian population during the First World War when they joined the Kaiser, and the Austrians, against the Allies, the British, French and Russians. In 1915 the Allies assaulted the Dardanelles and Gallipoli. From there, the Allies, had they succeeded, could have invaded Constantinople, toppled the Turkish government and forced their surrender. Gallant troops from Australia, New Zealand, and Britain died in horrifying numbers at Gallipoli, victims, not merely of the Turkish army, but decimated by disease, and sacrificed to leadership entirely inept. Among the English losses, the poet Rupert Brooke (... *there's some corner of a foreign field that is forever England...*) who with many others perished in western Turkey. To the east, particularly in the more isolated mountains and desert regions, Armenian men, women and children were massacred. But by 1923, it was all quiet on the Western Front, war-torn France and Belgium. Quiet too at Gallipoli. Quiet in the eastern deserts where Armenian bones bleached unburied.

It was not all quiet in Constantinople, a panoply of voices and languages and cultures. But after their return from the police station and after supper, and the little ones got down to sleep, it was quiet in the Kalpakian kitchen, Haroutune and Haigouhi, and her younger brother, Haigauz, their hands folded, sat. I can't imagine what they said. In truth, I can't imagine them talking at all.

This is not a failure of the imagination. It is not even a failure of language in that neither I, nor any of my cousins, not my mother, nor my aunts, none of us has any morsel of Armenian language. This is pervasive silence. Haroutune and Haigouhi enveloped their old country experience in a veil of silence, shrouded it in silence, buried it in silence. In America, the uniform cry of their lives was *assimilate assimilate*, but their Armenian experience, or if you wish, their Turkish experience, died before they did, asphyxiated in the silence that in our family was as thick and abstruse as smoke. Silence prevailed, became, in physical terms, not so much a gas like smoke, but a substance like ash, like grit, or lint or sand. At age eighty-four, and at the insistence of her daughter, Betty, my grandmother wrote in longhand "The Story of My Life," a document that is certainly interesting, descriptive though not detailed, and lacking any introspection. It lives up to a statement she once made in my hearing: *You cannot put in words your feelings. You can only describe the conditions. But how you feel, you cannot say.* She did indeed describe conditions, but how she felt, she did not say. Not ever. After she died in 1987, and certain artifacts and documents came to light, questions arose, incomplete questions, voices in the void. These documents that came to me—the already described passport, the ship manifest, the Declaration of an Alien About to Depart for the United States, the inventory of their household goods—these are *noisy* documents. Chatty, rife with gossip, possibility, with implication, if not understanding, illumination if not revelation. From these official pages arose a multitude of questions, but by then my grandmother had died, her silence unchallenged.

And who would have challenged her? Not any of us. She was a formidable woman. Not cold or angry or stolid as the words suggest in English, but rather, as the French use it, *formidable!* A tremendous force in her own right, a powerful presence, *formidable!* But until these documents and artifacts emerged, we never really guessed at the extent of her silence. After all, little bits of anecdote had been broken off the silence, shaped and often-told. These few stories, three in all, each has its indelible, obligatory exclamation point at the end! If they did not, they would not be amusing! And if they were not amusing, they would not have become stories! You see the point in print more easily. I have come to think of them as the Three Stories: the Cup of Coffee Story, the Hot Water Tap Story, and the Dumbbell Story.

Here is the Cup of Coffee Story: Armenian marriages were not love matches, but traditionally arranged between families. According to old country custom, marriage negotiations were conducted over a ritual that involved coffee, the sort of coffee known variously as Turkish coffee, or Armenian coffee, or Lebanese coffee, Greek coffee, whatever your ethnic background might be. That is: coffee beans ground to a fine powder, put on to boil in a long-handled pan, cooked till the froth rises, and poured correctly into demitasse cups, the foam just so. The mother of the prospective groom (and maybe his female relatives) come to the home of the prospective bride. She makes coffee. If the prospective groom's mother sips and says, *Ah, this coffee is good,* negotiations can go forward; if not, everything is off.

My grandmother was born Haigouhi Koulahksouzian in 1901. She lived in Adana, Turkey a prosperous city near the eastern Mediterranean where there was a large Congregationalist missionary presence that included a church, a hospital and the Adana Girls' Seminary. In April 1917 Haigouhi had graduated from this school which was run by American Congregationalist missionaries, women educated in America, serving abroad. The principal was a Miss Grace Towner (a woman who deserves her own biography and a place in the annals of courage that I alas, cannot give her here). How these students must have looked up to their teachers! But for Armenian girls, jobs as teachers were out of the question; the only possible future was marriage, even though, given the war and the years of mass killings, there were few Armenian men to marry. Indeed, traditionally, most Armenian girls would only have been educated in housewifely skills. But at the Adana Girls' Seminary Haigouhi had an American education, history, math, English language, French. After graduation she earned her keep at the school by teaching English grammar.

Haigouhi had an aunt who worked in a factory that made canvas for the Turkish war effort. This aunt was eager that

Haigouhi should meet the family of the young Armenian foreman in the factory. The aunt invited Haigouhi and the young man's mother for an afternoon visit. Haigouhi made the coffee. The mother sipped, said, *Ah, this coffee is good*, and smiled. Haigouhi obediently left the room so the mother and her aunt could discuss negotiations. But when the aunt asked Haigouhi about marrying him, Haigouhi had one question: could he read and write? No, he could not. *Forget it*, declared Haigouhi, *I can read and write four languages and I will not marry an illiterate man!*

This Cup of Coffee story was related throughout my family countless times, and always with the same vocal inflections signifying *Bravo, for the orphaned Haigouhi! She knew how to stand up for herself and her own worth!*

But there is no story with an exclamation point to tell us how Haigouhi felt, just two years earlier, in 1915, when Miss Towner came to her house and asked her parents if Haigouhi could become a boarding student at the American school instead of a day student. As part of a far-flung network of missionaries all over Turkey, Miss Towner would have known without doubt what was happening after April 1915 when in Constantinople the Turks rounded up Armenian leaders in every field, arrested them all, and executed most. All over Turkey, especially in the inland, hard-to-reach regions the Turks commanded the Armenians to leave their homes and property (no small consideration) to be "evacuated," marched into the deserts, to die of thirst and starvation. Miss Towner would have known this same fate lay ahead for the Adana Armenians as well.

Haigouhi herself might have known, at least guessed. She had vivid memories of 1909 when terrible massacres were perpetrated against the Adana Armenians. As an old woman she wrote this description:

When I was 8 years old, one Sunday afternoon I went to church with my twelve year old cousin. When the service was over, we heard some guns sounding and then – Turkish soldiers herded us and all the people coming out of the church to a park near the river. They kept us there overnight—we had no food or shelter. I remember cuddling with my cousin to keep warm. I was terribly scared and cried. In the morning, we were told the soldiers were waiting for their orders – either to throw all of us in the river or let us go. Fortunately, the orders came through to let us go. I don't remember why we went back to the church, but we did. I saw that the Turks had set the church on fire and saw the church bell tumbling down to the ground from the burning tower. When it fell it went deep into the ground. When I went home, my mother was at the neighbor's house where she had taken shelter from the Turks. When she heard me crying at the door—she knew it was me and she opened the door. The neighbor, who was an attorney, was not bothered by the Turks, because he wore a white Turkish head band, posing as a Turk himself and he told the soldiers, "What are you doing here, scaring the women and children?" (He had a wife and a daughter). The Turks left him alone. In the meantime, they (the Turks) had

looted our house (which was next door) and had even
stolen all our bread which we had baked the day before.

In 1915 Haigouhi's parents had two children living at home, fourteen year old Haigouhi, and ten year old Haigauz. Their elder daughter, Dudu, and elder son, Asdoor, had immigrated to America in 1907. Asdoor had accompanied Dudu on the long journey to Los Angeles where she married her fiancé, a Mr. Boyajian, the owner, by then, of a Santa Monica drug store. Asdoor eventually owned cigar stands on Pickering Pleasure Pier, and he sent money home to Adana monthly. The parents knew their elder children were safe in America. Perhaps the American school could protect their younger daughter from what lay ahead.

Thus, at fourteen Haigouhi parted with her parents forever. In that same late-in-life document my grandmother described this crucial, heart-wrenching event this way: "Miss Towner, Principal of the American school asked me to stay in that school as a boarding student." That is all. *You cannot put in words your feelings. You can only describe the conditions. But how you feel, you cannot say.*

As Haigouhi collected her few things, did her mother cling to her? Silence. Did her mother help her pack? Silence. Did her father hold her one last time? Silence. Did they weep? Silence. Did Haigouhi hug her ten-year-old brother, Haigauz? Did he cry? Silence. Did she know that given the sanctuary of the American school, she would live? Did she guess that they would die? Silence. Again, you can see in print how the silence engenders question marks, where the oft-told-stories require exclamation points! Never did my grandmother indicate anything of that leave-taking, not to her children, not to her grandchildren. She went with Miss Towner to the Adana Girls' Seminary, and there she lived, studied, and earned her keep waiting tables and making the French teacher's bed every day. The rest of them were marched into the desert, to starve or be killed, to die in any event.

Her younger brother did not die. Haigauz, about age ten, was rounded up with his parents and others, and "evacuated" into the eastern deserts. He watched his father die of starvation. His mother as well. He watched as the Kurds came and stripped the Armenian exiles. (Can one be an exile in one's own country? A refugee in the land one has always called home? Was it home? The desert where his father died, was that home?) The Kurds swept down and took from them all their clothing, which was all they had anyway, left them naked, dead. The Kurds took young Haigauz as a slave.

Haigauz's first owner used him as a shepherd boy. This man had a daughter who taught him the Kurdish language when they took the sheep to pasture daily. He ran away once, back to the Armenian encampment where he found unburied bones. Did he find his mother's body? We don't know. We only know the Kurd caught him, brought him back, sold him to another Kurd, a man with two contentious wives. He was a smart boy, Haigauz, a shrewd boy, so smart and shrewd that in time his relations with his owner deteriorated and one day the man tried to kill him, flung a knife at him; he carried this scar on his neck his whole life. Haigauz ran away, to the east, even further east and he changed his name to Ali. He spoke only Kurdish and he lived for five years on the run, cadging, begging, stealing, working, lying, living as best he could.

In 1978, in my grandmother's livingroom, Haigauz recounted these five years of his life into a tape recorder. On the tape we can hear the coffee cups chime on the saucers. The traffic from Olympic Boulevard, Los Angeles. Late in this recorded narrative Haigauz (who speaks in an even, hypnotic, singsong voice) ventures near the unsayable, beginning to recount his return to the Armenian encampment where he found the unburied bones. My grandmother interrupts him: *That's enough. We've heard enough. I've heard enough. It does no good now. That's enough.* Then she adds, as both edict and observation, *You cannot put in words your feelings. You can only describe the conditions. But how you feel, you cannot say.*

Okay, Haigauz replies. *Okay* was his favorite punctuating word. As he tells his story that afternoon, he always throws in the contemplative *Okay, what I gonna do?* After he ran away from the second Kurd, he traveled two hundred miles to the east, begging, stealing, dodging Kurds and Turks and Arabs. He stumbled onto an encampment of Kurdish workers building a railroad for the German army (the would-be Berlin-to-Baghdad railway that was so important to the German/Turkish war effort). He spoke Kurdish language and they sent him two tents down, to see the Turkish boss, to get work. Haigauz's telling of this tale indicates that Kurdish was his only language at this time—not the only language he dared to speak, but the only one he *could* speak, as though the other two languages, the home-language Armenian, and the street-language Turkish, had both been eradicated from memory. He got the job, and slowly his recollection of Turkish returned, which delighted the Turkish boss because he needed someone to translate for him to his Kurdish workers. He made this boy a sort of foreman, translating orders and told him to watch out when the Germans came around, to stay out of the way of the German officer in charge of the rail-building. Haigauz would recognize this particular officer because he rode a fine horse. Haigauz had a little dog (how or when he came by this dog, he does not say) and the dog had the bad sense to bite the leg of the German officer's horse. The Germans threw the boy and the dog into a tent that sufficed for a jail and told them to stay there. *Okay, these Germans, what they gonna do with me? Shoot me maybe. And I'm petting the dog, and I'm saying, you put me like this, you see, and I'm looking round the tent and I see nothing but dirt, and I went there, started digging and this dog just came over here and start digging, digging under the tent and we made enough room and slide under there and run. The dog too*, says Haigauz, adding, *But the dog left behind 'cause I didn't want to take care of him because I didn't have nothing to eat myself, what I gonna do with the dog?*

One wonders what he did with the dog. One wonders at their parting. But the dog vanishes from his story, from his life, which after that was *Walking every day, one place to the other, looking for something, somewhere, looking for something, someplace that we can live or do something.*

Haigauz lies, cheats, steals, befriends another orphaned Armenian boy, and under the name Ali, works for a cook in the Turkish army, goes into town to exchange money for the Turkish soldiers. And finally, after World War I staggers to its terrible close, Haigauz is picked up, sick, "with a high temperature—he was sitting in the rain under a tree in the wilderness," my grandmother wrote. Another story was that he was found sick, begging on the streets of Dörtyol (so he had clearly worked his way back toward Adana) by Near East Relief workers.

The Near East Relief workers' attempts to ameliorate the fate of orphans and survivors throughout the region were thwarted by a lack of supplies, lack of food, lack of sustenance, and frustrated continually by Turkish military and civilians from whom they had to secure permissions. James Barton's 1930 book, *Near East Relief 1915-1930* tries for restrained presentation of the obstacles they faced. (The footnotes are less restrained.) Barton details the plight of these pathetic children all over the Middle East; orphaned, sick, exhausted, some simply lying on the ground waiting to die. Relief workers collected these children, brought them to orphanages, did what they could by way of sustenance, medical attention, some small attempts at training or education. Haigauz was taken to a Foundling Home where he stayed for about nine months. The politics of this time, 1920, were internationally, politically, militarily, and culturally complex; they strain even the most astute mind which I do not claim to have. Suffice it here to say that the orphanage was going to close, and the children would be shipped to Jerusalem. In a last attempt to unite orphans with families, they published the names of all the orphans, and Haigauz Koulahksouzian was among them.

A friend of Haigouhi's saw his name and brought it to her attention. Haigouhi, married and a mother by now, wrote to the Foundling Home saying she was alive and wanted to be reunited with her brother. The Kalpakians hired a man "to go to the orphanage with clothes for Haigauz and 50 Turkish liras to the school for their services," she wrote in her eighties. "Then they released Haigauz to him to bring him to Adana to live with us. (I don't remember how much we paid the man.)" After all that, she says nothing of the reunion of brother and sister, orphaned, separated for years, neither knowing if the other had lived or died. Nothing. *You cannot put in words your feelings. You can only describe the conditions. But how you feel, you cannot say.*

II

The Kalpakians, my grandfather's people, were merchants and bankers, quite wealthy, so it came down to us. Rumors— like little wisps, like lint, or ash, or grains of sand—came down to us that they had had money. Rumor persisted, but silence prevailed and we never were told anything particular, save that until the First World War, the Kalpakians had lived in a beautiful home in the seaport city of Mersin. That wraith of rumor was only recently dusted off when in 2021, after my mother wrote her *Centennial Memoir*, we were contacted by the Krakirians, Kalpakian cousins, descendents of my grandfather's sister, Zabelle, of whom we had heretofore known nothing. They shed some new, much-needed light on this distant past.

In 1915 Haroutune's younger sister, Zabelle Kalpakian married Khatchadour Krakarian in Mersin. Khatchadour was a good deal older than Zabelle who was just nineteen or so. As the general manager, basically, president of the Ottoman Bank in Adana (the Ottoman Bank was effectively the central bank of the entire Ottoman Empire) Khatchadour had important connections in Turkey and abroad. If the Kalpakians were also in business or banking, perhaps that's how they connected socially with Khatchadour. One assumes this was an arranged marriage, as was the custom. Following Armenian traditions, after the wedding the bride left Mersin, and went to live with her husband's family, his widowed mother and his unmarried sister, in Adana. Armenian tradition also meant that the new bride would serve the groom's family in domestic work. In the household of a man in Khatchadour's high position, they no doubt had servants for domestic duties, and Zabelle, as an educated young lady from a wealthy family would not have been expected to do chores. However, the whole question of tradition was moot soon after they returned to Adana because Khatchadour Krakarian was swept up, arrested and imprisoned in the first wave of assaults against influential Armenian leaders. His young bride, alone with his old mother and his unmarried sister, must surely have been mad with worry, and she wrote anguished letters to her family in Mersin. At first her mother and her brother Haroutune came to her aid, but eventually the rest of the family followed, leaving the Mersin house to be confiscated by the Turks. All of the Kalpakians, seven in total, went to Adana, and moved in with Zabelle and the Krakirian women. How long Khatchadour was imprisoned, I do not know, but my Krakirian relatives tell me that on the day he should have been hanged, he was released. One can only imagine the torment this family endured, and the joy they must have felt at his release. Probably Khatchadour was spared because of his connections through the Ottoman Bank, but no doubt a great many bribes changed hands as well.

Probably more bribes changed hands shortly thereafter to keep them all from being rounded up and marched into the desert. More bribes yet to secure a job for Haroutune. Then in his twenties, Haroutune was ripe to be drafted into heavy labor for the Turkish army, as were many Armenian men. Instead, in August 1917 he was clerking in a dry goods store owned by a German when he met Haigouhi who, with two other young teachers, came in to do some shopping for the Adana Girls' Seminary.

In her "Story of My Life," my grandmother wrote: "When I met the young man — Haroutune, (Harry) he asked my name and where I lived. He went home and told his mother — 'today I met the girl I'm going to marry.' The next Monday, his mother came to school and told Miss Towner (my principal) that she wanted to see me because 'she was a friend of my parents.'" Maddeningly, Haigouhi says nothing of this interview. There is no Cup of Coffee story here! No mention of the groom's mother saying, *Ah, this coffee is good.* She immediately goes on: "Within one week, his father, and his brother-in-law came to school to see me with the same story. His parents had another girl in mind for him, but he was not interested." Again, she offers nothing further, no word whatever on her discussions with the Kalpakian men. One wonders if Miss Towner was present.

"The Story of My Life" continues: "Then, he (Haroutune) came to school himself to see Miss Towner and told her what his intentions were. Miss Towner told him— She (Haigouhi) still owes the school $50 for her room and board. He said he will pay it. When Miss Towner told me 'this man wants to marry you, but he belongs to the Apostolic Church, not the Congregational Church, you don't want to marry him.' I said, 'Yes, I do. It doesn't make any difference what church he belongs to.'"

We may thus assume that by then Haigouhi knew Haroutune could read and write; indeed, he could read and write several languages including French and Arabic. Miss Towner gave her consent; times were increasingly perilous, and the United States had entered the war in April 1917, so her status as an American missionary could imperil her fate and that of her students.

Miss Towner, with the Greek teacher from the Adana Girls' Seminary attended the wedding in October 1917 in the groom's family home, Armenian churches by that time having all been closed. Two wedding pictures have come down to us, one with the bride and groom, the bride wearing a wedding dress that I suspect belonged to Zabelle since Haigouhi, an orphan, coming from the school, would have had the clothes on her back and little else. And a second studio photograph with the bride and groom standing on either side of the groom's steely faced mother whose expression does not bode well for happiness.

As was the Armenian custom, Haigouhi moved in with her new husband's family. This meant that in the Krakirians' home, she, the new bride, joined Khatchadour and Zabelle who now had an infant son, Khatchadour's mother and sister, as well as seven Kalpakians. Thirteen of them in a house that, given Khatchadour's standing with the bank, was probably spacious, though perhaps not gracious given the ongoing war, and the uncertain fate of Armenians. Still, all of the Kalpakians were *alive*, all of them, including men (Haroutune and his brother Garabed) of military age. They had not been marched off into the desert with the other Adana Armenians. The significance of this fact is lost until it is placed in historical context. Of all the Armenians I have ever known in my life, the Kalpakians are the only ones who suffered *not so much as one casualty* during the Armenian Genocide. No one died. All were dispersed, true, but no one died, and that fact alone testifies to their wealth, their connections, and without doubt hefty bribes that changed from their Armenian hands into Turkish hands. The fact that they were all alive, given the perils, the horrors of those years, also testifies to some incredible constellation of lucky stars.

However grand the Krakirian home, by 1917 I expect the servants were gone. The new bride, Haigouhi, was a penniless orphan, educated, true, but so what? She was expected follow tradition and serve the groom's family domestically. The Kalpakian and Krakirian women apparently felt that Haigouhi was very much wanting in the domestic arts. Her American education at the Adana Girls' Seminary would not have endowed her with housekeeping skills beyond the making of beds. As a child she had helped her mother with the baking and the like, but trained to housekeeping? No. Haigouhi's in-laws criticized her sharply and often. In her eighties, writing "The Story of My Life" she described the experience like this: "I was delegated to do the ironing, house cleaning, knead the dough for bread, set the table, clear the table. I was constantly reminded that I didn't know how to cook, how to sew, didn't iron very well, etc., etc." Haigouhi did not take kindly to being ordered about, and being continually criticized. Perhaps her American education contributed to her independent streak. Certainly the famous Cup of Coffee story proves that even as a girl, she knew her own mind. She would have spoken up, possibly spoken out, at least to her husband. Within a few months she was pregnant, and this too might have contributed to her wish to escape the Kalpakian/Krakirian household. In "The Story of My Life" she says "So we lived with his folks for nine months and then we moved to our own place." In a different version, (this one typed and lightly edited by her daughter, Betty) she says they lived there "until we couldn't take it anymore." In this version she has a hand-written asterisk "They never forgave us." The "they" being perhaps just the Kalpakian parents, or possibly, the whole family, everyone living in that house. The asterisk, "never forgave," written some sixty-five years later, suggests that the split was angry all round.

The young couple moved out, but they remained in Adana. Haroutune's wages at the German's dry goods store would have supported them. Their eldest daughter was born in Adana, December 26th 1918. They named her Angaghouhi (Independence, or Liberty) because Haroutune, a scholarly man, interested in history and politics, was thrilled with the post-war prospect that an actual Armenian homeland might come as a result of peace. The Armistice had been declared November 11, 1918 just weeks before her birth.

But like everything else in the post-war world, these political questions were in flux, and the fates of millions decided by a bunch of old men haggling over the Treaty of Versailles in Paris. In 1919 the Middle East was carved up into fiefdoms for voracious, competing European powers. The Ottoman Empire was dead, but a new nationalism was rising in Turkey, and with it civil unrest among different political factions, more fighting, more bloodshed, more civilian deaths, to say nothing of the Spanish influenza pandemic that gripped the whole world. In short, amid the whole unthinkable morass of post-war Turkey, any Armenian who could flee, did.

Into the diaspora go the Armenians! A people with two thousand years of culture and no country, people with their own church and language, music, literature, art and architecture, and no homeland in which to build or create or practice. They dispersed like smoke.

My grandfather would never again see his parents or his brothers and sisters who fanned out across the Middle East and Europe. Khatchadour and Zabelle Krakirian, and their children went first to Haifa in Palestine, and later to Jerusalem. Their youngest son was born there in 1929, and Khatchadour died there in 1944. Zabelle and her children and grandchildren would eventually scatter, often hurriedly, and at the behest of wars, among the cities of Aleppo and Damascus in Syria, and Beirut, Lebanon. Haroutune's parents, one sister and his two brothers, Nishan and Garabed got French passports that allowed them to go to Romania. The Kalpakian parents died there in the 1930s. (Haroutune kept in touch with his brother, Nishan by letter. My mother remembers black-bordered envelopes arriving in the 1930's with foreign stamps.) Nishan and Garabed each got married and had children in Romania, but on the eve of the Second World War, Romania expelled anyone who did not have a Romanian passport. Displaced again, they went to France where they suffered under the Nazi Occupation.

Nearly a hundred years would pass before there was any sort of reconnection among the Kalpakian descendents. In 2016 Nishan's granddaughter, Astrid Kaloustian reached out to us when she found Helen Kalpakian's "The Story of My Life" on the internet. My mother, Peggy in her nineties, and Nishan's daughter, Arminee Kaloustian in her eighties, were the only ones of all that generation still alive. Neither could speak the other's language. Arminee could speak Armenian, but my mother could not. The rest of us communicated in makeshift French and English, facilitated by Astrid's excellent English, and my cousin Patty Stephenson who taught French for many years. In 2018 Astrid and her family flew from Paris to Los Angeles and met us in person, a joyous reunion that included my sister, my sons, my daughter-in-law, and my little grand-daughter. In 2020, because of my mother's *Centennial Memoir*, we were able to connect with the Krakirians, Zabelle's descendents, and though they live in Southern California, Covid-19 has kept us from meeting in person.

III

In November 1921 Haroutune, Haigouhi, their little daughter, Angagh and Haigauz were physically expelled from Adana. "In the night," wrote my grandmother, "and we were all hurried to get on the train, Turkish soldiers pushing us with bayonets to get on the train like a cattle car." These few words were all Helen Kalpakian ever had to say of their leaving Adana. The train took them east, to Syria. She had nothing whatever to say of the four months (say, November to February or early March) they lived in Alexandrette, a French-mandated city in those uneasy years following the Great War. A pall, the smoke of silence, hangs over their Syrian experience.

What did they carry with them when they were crowded onto those cattle cars? Haigouhi certainly packed up her diploma from the American school; it was part of their declared goods when they came to the US, as was her graduation photograph. Where did they live in Alexandrette? What did they use for money? She never disclosed to any of us any word of those four months in Alexandrette, Syria. However, Haigauz in his taped conversation in 1978 amid the coffee cups and traffic sounds from Olympic Boulevard, mentions that Haroutune during those four months "took a trip to the Holy Land." I always wondered: why would he leave his pregnant wife and little daughter in a foreign country, probably fairly hostile country under the protection of a boy who was no doubt still traumatized, mentally and physically? Was Haigouhi angry at being left? Where was she left? A hotel? An apartment? Now that I know Zabelle and her husband had dispersed to Haifa, I wonder if perhaps Haroutune went to see his sister one last time. (That presupposes that Haroutune knew she had gone to Haifa, that he still had contact with his family, even if he and his wife remained unforgiven.) Or perhaps "the Holy Land" meant Jerusalem. Of what Haroutune saw, or where he went, or what he thought of it, we have nothing; the whole trip, the purpose remains shrouded in mystery.

Then on the tape my grandmother gets up to brew more coffee, and Haigauz tells an unexpected anecdote of her and a fortune teller in Alexandrette. For half a loaf of bread, a fortune teller would read her palm. *Ah*, she told Haigouhi, *You will move again soon and you are expecting another child.* It probably took no great foresight to divine either of these, but no one present listening to Haigauz can imagine Helen Kalpakian (prudent, literal-minded, hard-working, no-nonsense) holding out the palm of her hand—much less half a loaf of bread—to a fortune teller!

When the French left Alexandrette, so did the Kalpakians. They boarded a ship, the *Bukovina*, in March, 1922 —
Haigouhi hugely pregnant—and crossed the Mediterranean,
westward towards Constantinople. They steamed through
the Aegean blue sea, the Greek isles, along all those ancient
beaches with all their ancient names: Rhodes, Léros, Sa-
mos, and Patmos where Saint John the Divine was said to
have written the Book of Revelation. Surely it must have
seemed to this family, to Europeans everywhere, that the
Four Horsemen of the Apocalypse had spent themselves
during the Great War and the influenza epidemic that followed. The *Bukovina* steamed up the Turkish coast, toward
Gallipoli and the Dardanelles—where New Zealand and
Australian soldiers died in 1915. Did Haroutune stand on
the steamer deck and wonder, as they passed the Dardanelles and all those foreign graves, how many Armenians
might have lived if the Allies had triumphed here? If the
Allies had taken Constantinople in 1915 and effectively
knocked Turkey out of the War? The Turks had accomplished their systematic annihilation of the minority Armenian population behind the curtain of war, just as Hitler
would, a generation later, seek to exterminate the Jews.

If anyone wondered these things, it would have been Haroutune. He was a dapper, bookish man, shrewd, cheerful
and charming. I cannot imagine Haigouhi wondering any
such thing. Speculation was never in her nature, imagination utterly outside her purview. Besides, one week after
their arrival in Constantinople, she gave birth to another
daughter on March 26, 1922, my mother, born Pakradouhi

Kalpakian. Haroutune went to work for a cousin who had an importing business.

Their eighteen months in Constantinople pass (like much else) in a veil of silence save for one anecdote that my grandmother describes with (what feels like) a bit of glee, testifying again to the fact that Haigouhi Kalpakian always knew her own mind.

My husband's uncle who was a textile manufacturer in Manchester, England had come to Istanbul and was looking for someone to send to Batoom, Russia, to open a branch for him there. He thought Haroutune would be the ideal person to send, so his uncle asked him. My husband accepted his offer and signed a contract to go to Russia. His uncle told him—"In England it's customary that a man's wife sign the contract, too", so he told him—"Take it home and let your wife sign it too." He brought it home and was so happy that we would be going to Russia. He said, "We're going to Russia." I said, "We are? Do you know the Russian language?" He said, "No." I said, "I don't either. Do you know any one there – or about the climate there, or the way they run business?" (This was 1922). It was only two years after the Bolshevik government had taken over Russia.) He said, "No, but we'll learn." I said, "I am not going to sign the contract—why don't we go to America, where I have a brother, and a married sister and I know a little English." He was disappointed, but he took the contract back unsigned. I have been thankful that I didn't sign it. We wrote to my sister and she and her husband sent

us an affidavit and we were given permission by the
American Consulate in Istanbul to leave for America

My mother always says seeing pictures of toothless Russian babushkas, their heads swathed, their features gaunt,
their bodies wrapped in heavy overcoats, makes her bless
her mother's foresight. How different would their lives
have been in Russia! (For context, the Russian Revolution
and civil wars went on for another ten years, followed by
Stalin's brutal Five Year Plans and purges and then the Second World War. Whew!) That Haigouhi prevailed, and they
went to America, even though Haroutune had the promise
of work in Russia, reflects, I think, not only the strength of
my grandmother's personality, her character, but the fun-
damental partnership of their long marriage. They worked
side by side in all their endeavors for over forty years, a
uniquely balanced union, not at all the patriarchal model
one associates with old country men and subservient wives.

IV

But many more hurdles lay between the Kalpakians and
leaving for America. Before they could even begin the immigration formalities commemorated in their 1923 passport, letters must go back and forth between the Kalpakians
in Constantinople, and Haigouhi's brother, Asdoor, now
known as Arthur Clark, her sister Dudu and her sister's
husband, John Boyd in California. Not surprisingly, none of
these letters survive. And if they did, who could read them?
They would have been written in Armenian, a language
that has its own alphabet. Nothing, not even a fragment
of a tale, has come down to us about Art and Dudu's feel-

ings, their eagerness, or resistance to the Kalpakians' letter requesting sponsorship. Did they feel joy? Misgivings? We have only the indubitable fact that they complied with the Kalpakians' request.

By 1923 Hovaness and Dudu Boyajian had become Mr. and Mrs. John Boyd. Asdoor Koulahksouzian had become Arthur Clark. (The family name, Koulahksouzian means, I'm told, "the one without an ear," probably commemorating some ancient anguish.) They were naturalized American citizens, sporting their new names, much as they might have worn boutonnieres, something fresh and decorative. They all lived together along with the Boyd's two teenage children in a beautiful ten room house with an acre of garden, 905 Harding Avenue, Venice California. They were well established. John Boyd by now owned several drug stores in Santa Monica, and Art Clark had cigar stands on the Pickering Pleasure Pier.

Did Art quit sending money to his parents in Adana when word seeped out of Turkey of death marches for the Armenians? After, say, headlines in the *New York Times*, August and September, 1915 spoke boldly of the horrors there? Did Art and Dudu, from their sunny, palm-lined California porch, did they tremble for the family in eastern Turkey? Did they, given the dearth of information during the Great War, know that their parents and little brother, Haigauz had been forced into the desert? Did they know that Haigouhi had been spared by living at the American school? Did they know she had married? That Haigauz was alive, and reunited with her? No one ever said.

Asdoor Koulahksouzian had fled Turkey under unusual circumstances. Hovanness Boyajian (soon to become John Boyd) had been Asdoor's English teacher at a boy's school in Tarsus, Turkey. He had (apparently) come to Adana with his student, met Dudu, and fell in love. Though Hovanness was already planning to go to America, they became engaged. Once he had completed pharmacist's school he would sent for her, and they would marry in America. In 1907 Dudu packed her bags. She had a steamship ticket to leave out of Mersin. Reluctant to send a girl, barely nineteen years alone on a journey that far, the family decided Asdoor should go with her. However, Asdoor, at twenty-three was of military age, and forbidden to leave Turkey. The story of his daring escape has come down to us: Dudu, her papers in order, boarded the steamer in Mersin. Asdoor waited till it pulled away from the dock, and swam out to it, making a successful escape. (Presumably Dudu had enough money with her to pay his fare once he had been hauled out of the sea.)

Back in Adana the family suffered for his success. Haigouhi and Haigauz (ages six and two at the time) spent two days in hiding at the Congregationalist minister's house when Turkish police came to her parents' home, searching for Asdoor, and roughly interrogated the parents who knew nothing of Asdoor's flight. Nothing. He was gone. Their daughter, Dudu, had gone to America to marry. They knew that.

There is a photograph of Haigouhi's mother, Ysabet, and Dudu taken just before their parting in 1907. A stained and sepia, heartbreaking photograph. You can see in their eyes, they know they will never meet again. They hold hands and stare forward, the girl's young face expressionless, the mother's brows twisted with sorrow. This is the only photograph Haigouhi had of either of her parents, and clearly she had this one because Dudu had a copy. In "The Story of My Life" Helen Kalpakian writes "My parents put all our family pictures in a box and buried them in the dirt under our house in Adana [in 1915]. They hid these pictures because they didn't want the Turks to know and identify family members." They buried their pictures in Adana, Turkey, but their bodies are buried in Los Angeles, California. Dudu and Art died within months of each other in 1939 and 1940. Helen and Haigauz died within months of each other in 1987.

In 1923 John Boyd and Arthur Clark vowed before a Los Angeles notary that the Kalpakians and Haigauz would not become a public nuisance, nor a charity. They sent this notarized voucher to the Kalpakians in Constantinople.

Once he received it, Haroutune filled out Form 228, the *Declaration of an Alien About To Depart for the United States,* before "Th. Murphy, American vice-consul in Constantinople." (I picture Mr. Murphy pale and dyspeptic, sitting behind a broad desk littered with official stamps.) In this declaration Haroutune Kalpakian solemnly swore that he intended to stay in America for good, that he was joining his wife's family who were already American citizens. He had the notarized voucher from his brothers-in-law, John Boyd, and Arthur Clark to prove it. In gathering these required documents, booking passage, filling out forms at the American Consulate, Haroutune and Haigouhi and Haigauz (and the little girl and the babe in arms) stood in endless queues. They paid the obligatory fees (and the just-as-obligatory bribes). They tolerated the endless delays and frustrations of getting their immigration papers in order, all the while silently framing the unfamiliar syllables, *Pickering Pleasure Pier Pickering Pleasure Pier.*

Did Haigauz, the boy who had been a slave, did he believe a pleasure pier could exist? Did Haigouhi? The young woman in the passport picture clearly does not believe in pleasure piers. And when they returned at night to 46 rue Patchadji, and walked up the three flights, and ate their evening meal off the four little plates (blue on the bottom, white on the top), their spoons clanking, did they wonder—perhaps more to the point, did they dare—to speak, to form the words, *Pickering Pleasure Pier?* Did they try to imagine the waves rushing under the high wooden boardwalk, or the foam swirling around tarred pilings where unlovely barnacles cling, slaves to the tide? Did they ask themselves if gulls soared high overhead, if moths zapped themselves silly against the electric lights? Cigar stands on the Pickering Pleasure Pier? Do the shelves gleam with candy bars and cigarettes? What else is on the Pickering Pleasure Pier? A dance pavilion? A tinny orchestra? Food stalls? Fortune tellers? Among them, these people spoke Armenian, Turkish, Kurdish, French, English, Arabic, and some Greek, but honestly, were there words for such vanities in any language they could possibly have spoken? Were there words at all? Or did the silence already reign?

V

By July 5, 1923, only one thing remained to be accomplished before they could leave for America: Form 139, to be completed before Mr. H. Brumley, another American vice-consul. This was the *Declaration of a Manufacturer, Owner, or Duly Authorized Agent of Either, Covering Goods Shipped Without Sale.* Haroutune Kalpakian swore (duly) he would not sell any of these goods; they were household effects only. The goods were to be shipped to his cousin's in-laws the Issakoolians, (ah, the uses of the diaspora!) rug merchants on Broadway in New York. For a fee of $2.50 paid in stamps, H. Brumley believed Haroutune Kalpakian. (One wonders if the Americans picked up the casual habits of bribery; odd, how money is the truly universal language.) Every item in these three bales is carefully itemized, its worth noted in Turkish piasters, its value calculated by Mr. Brumley. Only two items had zero value: a small pack of photographs, and one Diploma, American School, although these were in fact, the most valuable things they declared. (Not that they took with them, as the reader will see, but that they declared; there is a difference.) The photographs were irreplaceable. The diploma from the American school meant my grandmother spoke English, indeed, that she had an American education that would allow them to *assimilate assimilate* far more easily than most immigrants.

The inventory itself is three pages long, two columns each. The wonder to me is that there was so much. They had only been married since 1917, had fled Adana in the night on cattle cars, and lived four months in Syria, just over a year in Constantinople where Haroutune worked in a relative's rug import business. Nonetheless they had this much to pack, ship and declare? The inventory itself supports my grandfather's oath that these are household goods: 60 collars for men (600 piasters), 41 pairs of stockings (30 piasters), one cap velvet (50 piasters), 1 brilliant bedstead belt (100 piasters), 6 pairs of gloves (70 piasters), 24 chemises, bodices and drawers (1200 piasters), 27 books (300 piasters), 2 paintings (100 piasters). I cannot help but wonder: what possible paintings were these, so cheap they cost less than the sixty collars for men? Which twenty-seven books did he ship? One package envelopes (30 piasters), 2 white curtains (75 piasters), 22 napkins, 1 tablecloth and 9 baby hats. They declared many things enigmatic to me: 1 impermissible for women? Two yards of tanjib, 3 tepsi, 1 petrole ojak, 2 tenjeres, 1 copying machine (60 piasters), 3 kelpetin and keser? Apart from those enigmatics, so much here is pathetic: one piece of sponge (20 piasters), 1 broom (10 piasters), 4 pieces of soap, some thread for stockings, one little box each tea and coffee, 1 kilo sugar, 2 kilos bulgur, 12 cups for tea and 4 little plates. (These little tin plates, blue on the bottom, white on the top, are dented and chipped, but they do not break, and they remain in my possession a century later.)

In terms of money, the most valuable things the Kalpakians shipped were rugs. Many rugs. All three bales were wrapped in rugs and there were rugs inside the bales, and these old country rugs, itemized separately, totaled many thousand piasters.

But what is not on this declaration is any jewelry whatever. Not a single ring or pin or bracelet, though we know they brought such things because they gave each of their four daughters two old country gold bracelets on their wedding days. But there was also a sapphire ring, a gold ring with three diamonds, a gold ring with two diamonds and a ruby, gold and diamond earrings, a gold oblong ring with many small diamonds. These items were the remaining personal property of Helen Clark Kalpakian when she died in 1987. No one in her entire family knew that she possessed these things. No one had ever before seen them.

The jewelry remaining in my grandmother's estate after her death (those final salutes to silence) was all appraised as having primarily antique value and judged to be over a century old: old country, old workmanship, old stones, old everything. However, no such jewelry is declared on this old inventory. On the inventory, however, they did declare 4 cache-corsets (100 piasters). I can well imagine the uses to which a cache-corset might be put. Perhaps the Romanov women were wearing cache-corsets: when the Bolsheviks executed them in 1917. The story is that bullets ricocheted all over, astonishing the Romanovs' executioners who found on their corpses that the women had sewed jewels to their bodices. Jewels insufficient finally to protect them, or to buy their way out of Russia, or even to prevent their being shot. But enough to stun their executioners.

In my grandmother's cache-corset (never mind she was pregnant again), and, I suspect, also sewed into her pockets and the seams of her clothing, were these rings and earrings, bracelets and brooches, the last perhaps eight or twelve of which turned up (undeclared) after her death. My grandmother was a very organized woman; at age eighty-two she arranged all her personal property, marking with masking tape on the bottom of each piece of furniture what was to go to whom. She arranged her will, and her papers, deeds, insurance, everything as though she was going on a long journey (to that Undiscovered Country where mortals are foreign and denied entry). She noted and accounted for everything except these rings, the last of the jewelry they had brought, undeclared. She took her silence to the grave and the rest of us were left to wonder not only how the Kalpakians might have come by these exquisite jewels, but how many others had they parted with, and why.

Clearly, with this much jewelry, and so many rugs, the Kalpakians were not impoverished, but they came third class just the same. To save money. They sailed on a Greek ship, the *SS Constantinople*, delayed at sea by mechanical failure, bobbing in the Atlantic for a day, arriving at Ellis Island, New York, one day later than scheduled, August 2, 1923.

I try to imagine what emotions must have rippled through these five among the huddled masses. Did Haroutune lift up little Angagh to his shoulder and say in whatever of his many languages he chose, *See, look! There is the Statue of Liberty!* Did he take the toddler Pakradouhi from her mother's arms and hold her up, and shout the same, perhaps in French, *Voila! Nous arrivons! Amerique!* Did he and Haigouhi and Haigauz get misty thinking of all and who they had left behind, and what yet lay ahead? I picture Haroutune, his arm around his wife's shoulders, jubilant and eighteen year old Haigauz, and the little girls soaking up the energy and excitement that must surely have run rampant in third class. They arrived at Ellis Island on August 2, the day of President Harding's funeral so all federal offices were closed. The passengers disembarked from the ship first class first, then second class, then third.

Imagine their increasing horror as the passengers were processed, because by the time officials got to third class, the quota—recently established quotas to keep in check the number of immigrants from southern Europe—had been filled and these five (and no doubt the rest of third class) were denied entry. They were allowed off the ship at Ellis Island; they were inspected, and had their health cards filled out, but they were not allowed to stay. Their passports are marked "Deported." They could see the Statue of Liberty, but after a few days they were herded back into the bowels of the ship.

In the silence that surrounds my family's past, we hear no tears, no gnashing, no moaning, no wailing, no swearing over their being deported, not a single curse to register all that hope and time and effort expended into devastating failure. We hear a funny story! The second of the Three Stories, The Hot Water Tap Story. The sole bit of this experience broken off, supplied with an exclamation point and told to amuse the children was the story of my grandmother's being so happily surprised when she turned on the tap at Ellis Island—and out came hot water! Hot running water! Imagine that!

This—the hot running water!—is the sole anecdote to emerge from that experience: five people (five and a half if you count Elizabeth Kalpakian born January 18, 1924) deported. The Kalpakians' was a one-way passport out of Turkey, so they could not return there, nor did they wish to; they had no old home, no home at all. However, the steamship company had an agreement with the US Government: they must carry back to the point of origin anyone Immigration deemed unfit to enter. (Usually this was the elderly, the lame, the mad, the criminal, or senile, but in the Kalpakians' case, they were the merely superfluous.) As the ship was a Greek liner, the Kalpakians went to Greece and their passport is duly stamped on 31 August 1923 to indicate they were provisionally admitted to Piraeus, Greece. My grandmother later wrote "The Greek government took us in because we were on a Greek Steamship Line with the understanding that we must leave on the next boat going to America. We stayed two weeks in Greece."

Where? In a hotel fronting the harbor? Camped in a set of rooms that opened onto a narrow street? Her account mentions that they ate only tomatoes, onions and bread for those two weeks, adding that she could hardly eat at all, feeling sick from pregnancy. What did they do for those two weeks? Did they walk the harbor? Did their eyes strain against the sunshine? Did Haroutune stand in more queues, offer more bribes, part with more of their cached jewelry (because they were not allowed to take money out of Turkey) in order to buy new tickets, book new passage. Second class. No more costly economies.

You cannot put in words your feelings. You can only describe the conditions. But how you feel, you cannot say.

Oh, but how their spirits must have sunk while in Piraeus. How their fears must have mounted. How their sense of being untethered, not simply from the past, but from the future, must have deprived them of sleep, and gnawed at their dreams when they did sleep. Did they, Haigouhi and Haroutune, speak of these fears, whisper between themselves as they lay in whatever bed they might have found in Piraeus? I know no answers to these questions, and probably, had I had the sense to ask them of my grandmother while she was alive, I still would have no answers. *You cannot put in words your feelings. You can only describe the conditions. But how you feel, you cannot say.* That or something very like it would have been her reply. All I can add now is that there have been times in my life I have taken heart to know that I have come from people who crossed the Mediterranean and Atlantic three times in three months, desperate people, perhaps, but dreaming just the same of better future that must surely lie just ahead, out of sight, over the unknowable horizon that stretched across the ocean in every direction.

VI

On September 13 they boarded the *SS Canada*, a French ship, to make one more sweep across the Mediterranean and the Atlantic. They next appear to me on the *Manifest of Alien Passengers for the United States Immigration Officer at the Port of Arrival, Providence, Rhode Island, October 1, 1923, page 90*. This manifest is a wonderful document: noisy, convivial, intimate, expressive, evocative. There are eleven people on page 90, mostly women: Armenians, Jews, Greeks, Romanians. There are the fianceés, two Greeks and an Armenian, young women in their early twenties, Sourpig Hartounian to marry a man living at 207 East 29th Street, New York City; Helene Karakassi to marry a man who lives in Toronto; Androniki Manolakaki to marry a man whose name has already been anglicized to James Michael, in Rocks, Pennsylvania. Androniki is illiterate, as are the two Romanians, a mother and daughter, Rona, sixty-five and Mathilda, thirty-nine, going to join Mathilda's husband, Maier Zammer at 1208 Adams Street, Brownsville, Texas. In an official hand it's noted that Rona is senile. Was she? Or did this merely mean that Rona gibbered in Romanian, that she could comprehend nothing, no sign, no instructions, that she wept without reason, looked confused and was elderly? Also there are two Jewish sisters going to join a brother in Montreal, Refka Cohen, age thirty-six, a teacher, who, the manifest tells us, speaks English and her sister, Cencha Cohen, twenty-five.

This manifest momentarily breaks the silence. The manifest tells us what Mathilda and Rona and Refka looked like, at least I know their height and coloring, their complexions, their eyes and hair. And I can hear their voices: the babble of second class, where Sourpig could speak Armenian at last without fear of reprisal, where Refka might have practiced her English with my grandmother, where Rona might still have sung in Romanian despite her having come most recently from Smyrna, Turkey. (Or what was left after the burning destruction of Smyrna in 1922: ash, cinder, death, dust, and ruin.) Perhaps all these women, whatever their language, helped to amuse my mother (now a toddler, nineteen months) or Angagh, a sturdy five-year-old, amused them in the way that children can be, without language of any sort, with rag dolls, or shadows on a wall. Perhaps the fiancées compared fiancé stories (how different will Rocks, Pennsylvania be from Crete?) and perhaps young Helene Karakassi flirted with Haigauz who was nineteen, though on his papers he is made to be younger so he could travel at a cheaper fare. Perhaps my grandfather told Mathilda his parents had gone to Romania, and perhaps all these people patched together their brief, forced camaraderie in any language that came literally to hand—gestures, or expressions, smiles, laughter. Or, perhaps these women were not given to laughter, but like my grandparents and Haigauz, were human debris in the wake of the First World War, exiles, refugees, looking *for something somewhere, looking for something, someplace that we can live or do something.*

On embarking Helene Karakassi told Immigration she had eight dollars, Sourpig Haroutunian had thirty five dollars, and each of the Cohen sisters had fifty dollars. Androniki had twenty dollars, and the Romanian women between them had three hundred. My grandfather had $735. An incredible sum! Where did this money come from? I am especially intrigued since they could not take money out of Turkey, so it must have been exchanged in Piraeus. (Rings, bracelets removed from the cache-corset?)

Immigration then asked them the name and address of their closest relatives in the country from whence they had come. All these women have long, chatty answers from which I can discern enough to imagine the homes they left behind. After the Kalpakians' name, there is a pathetic, *Nobody.* They had no one in Greece, no one in Turkey; they had only the Pickering Pleasure Pier which must have beckoned and winked at them, possibilities now so close as they filed off the SS Canada.

Question 26: Have you ever been deported from the United States? All the women say *No* but my grandparents say *Yes, August 1923*, and no doubt my grandmother's schoolgirl English stood the test of explanations, how they had been deported because of quotas and not for any of the reasons listed below: had they ever been in prison, insane, or supported by charity? *No.* Were they anarchists? *No.* Were they polygamists? *No.* Did they believe in or advocate the violent overthrow of the US Government? *No.* Were they deformed or crippled and if so, the nature and length of time and cause. *No.* Question 20: Whether alien intends to return to country whence he came? *No.* Question 21: Whether alien intends to become citizen of the United States. *Yes.* Question 22: Length of time alien intends to reside in the United States. My grandfather replied *indefinitely* and in the line behind him, the fiancées and the Cohen sisters took his cue, and by their names it is also written, *indef.* But when the immigration officer asked this question of the Romanian women, both illiterate and one suspected of senility, two women en route to Brownsville, Texas, their reply is a heartbreaking, *always.*

After they departed the *SS Canada,* these voices disappear into another kind of diaspora, the North American diaspora, and now, of course, one hundred years later, all of these women have gone to that last home, that last country from whence no one returns. Perhaps they, like my grandparents, kept their silence to the end, but here on this manifest, their voices rise off the page, ascend out of the past and I hear everything. I understand, regardless of their language, the hope and fear, the leaving home and going home, all at the same time.

No one was going as far west as Ocean Park, California. No one had the ineffably romantic destination of Pickering Pleasure Pier. My grandmother's terse account written in her eighties only noted that the Kalpakians "landed in Providence, Rhode Island, October 1, 1923, 12:15 am." They had missed the last train to New York, and sat all night in the Providence train station. Did they sleep on the benches?

Did the children fuss? Were they hungry? Did they speak? Did they dare to speak? I imagine them sitting, their backs to the wall while a night janitor pushes a broom past them, silently sweeping up the refuse of other travelers.

Once in New York they contacted the Issakoolians, the distant semi-sort-of-cousins-in-laws to whom they had shipped their three bales of household goods all wrapped in rugs. Mr. Issakoolian arranged for them to stay in a hotel. The plumbing is all that emerges from the experience. How impressed my grandmother was to have a bathroom in the room! A bathtub and the hot running water! Hot water and a flush toilet and a bath tub right there in your room! We're never told how she felt when she finally closed that bathroom door, ran that hot water in the tub and took off her heavy traveling clothes from her pregnant body, the cache-corset with all the goods they had failed to declare, the rings and brooches that had bit into her flesh and caused her to cry, with pain, fear, with anxiety, to cry now with relief, with joy, to cry for the ones who were left unburied, for the siblings she was going to see after fifteen years, for the husband and brother and two daughters brought to this safety, for the child she was carrying. Did she turn on the hot water, and let it thunder into the tub to cover up the sound of her weeping? In all my life I never saw my grandmother cry. At my grandfather's funeral, she alone remained dry-eyed.

The next morning Mr. Issakoolian took them in a taxicab to the train station for the journey to Los Angeles. When the cab suddenly stopped and then started again, they were afraid that something was wrong. Mr. Issakoolian explained about traffic lights. They had never seen a traffic light. My grandmother's account is careful to note that Mr. Issakoolian got the tickets, though they paid their own fares (and paid for the hotel). Mr. Issakoolian bought them some ham sandwiches for the journey, and since she did not note otherwise, these were probably a gift.

From New York they rode the train across the country, five days, from which experience, no observation, no anecdote, not so much as a word arises. Not how they managed more food once past the ham sandwiches. How they managed the on-board bathrooms. (How to read MEN or LADIES or bathrooms at all.) How to change the toddler's diapers. What to do with the dirty diapers? What were their thoughts on the vast prairies? The mountains? What did they think when they stepped off the train in Los Angeles, and searched the crowd for people they had not seen in fifteen years, people that Haroutune had never before met.

John and Dudu Boyd and Art Clark met them at the train station, and they all got into the Boyd's car. (*What is this? They own their own car? Really? Can this be?*) According to my grandmother's terse written record Art and the Boyds took them home to 905 Harding Street in Venice, the grand ten room house where they had a party for them that very night. (No thought to how exhausted they might be? How undone? How overwhelmed?) Again, not a single anecdote arises from this reunion of people who had not seen one another in some fifteen years, years in which Art and Dudu must surely have feared their siblings had died in the onslaught of violence visited upon Armenians. And the immigrants themselves, did they weep to be embraced, weak with deliverance to be out of Turkey at last? *You cannot put in words your feelings.* And my grandparents never did. Not so much as a wisp of a word of this reunion. And now, of course at this great distance in time, one hundred years later, I kick myself because I never asked.

VII

Haigauz for a time had a room in the Boyd's big house. Haigouhi and Haroutune and their two daughters lived in the two-room gardener's cottage on the property. In January 1924, some three months after their arrival, another daughter was born there, Elizabeth, known as Betty, their first American child. A snapshot of Haigouhi in 1924 shows a young woman with a long mane of dark hair wearing an ankle-length dress and a shapeless apron. Two years later, another snapshot taken in the same setting shows a young woman, her hair cut short, flawlessly marcelled, wearing a sassy knee-length skirt, pale stockings and shoes with heels. Haigouhi had become Helen Kalpakian. Haroutune became Harry. I was in my twenties before I knew they ever had any other names at all.

Helen had her schoolgirl English, but Harry had none. His first job, working in a Kewpie doll factory, mercifully, did not demand much English. I imagine him painting the pink faces, the rosebud lips of these tawdry dolls with a sense of bewilderment. He studied English at night school, Manual Arts High, an experience that must have taxed him in every way since he did not even know the letters of the alphabet. Shortly thereafter he went to work for Art Clark at one of the cigar stands on the Pickering Pleasure Pier. Art Clark probably coached him with sufficient limited English to get by. *Cigarette? Cigar? Candy? Thank you!* could be easily augmented with a smile, and some hand gestures, and getting to know the logos. *Lucky Strike? Chesterfield?* This became the basis for the third of my grandmother's stories, the Dumbbell Story.

My grandfather was behind the counter of the cigar stand, and young flapper came by. She did not want cigarettes or candy. All she wanted was change for a dollar. Harry had no idea what she meant. *Cigarette? Cigar? Candy? Thank you!* was all he could repeatedly say, pointing to his various wares. This girl was disgusted, and before she sauntered off, she sniffed, "Dumbbell." Harry came home and asked Helen, "What means dumbbell?" But her proper schoolgirl English was not equal to this expression. Finally Art had to tell them. Everyone had a good laugh over this. The story, as it came down to us gently paves over the pathos, the pain, the anxiety of making one's way, indeed, making a living in a country where he did not know the language or the customs. When Angagh's kindergarten teacher came to their home and told them their daughter was falling behind at school, that Angagh could learn more easily if she spoke English at home, husband and wife made a pact. After that, whatever Armenian or Turkish passed between them was never again said in the hearing of the children. English only. *Assimilate, assimilate.* Harry's English came to be good, but not fluent, his words always heavily accented, and he always encouraged his daughters to correct his pronunciation.

I imagine Harry in those very early days of their arrival, gazing out at the Pacific from behind the counter of the cigar stand on the Pickering Pleasure Pier, pondering how far he had come from Mersin and the Mediterranean. When Harry was a very old man, retired from the grocery business, he asked his wife to drive him several times a week to the park in Santa Monica. He would get out of the car and walk to the bluff overlooking the ocean, sit on a bench, and stay there for hours staring at the vast Pacific. My grandmother waited in the car. She had seen enough ocean.

The Kalpakians lived in the gardener's cottage for three and a half years. They moved out following a family quarrel with John Boyd of which no one ever spoke in any detail, though clearly, it was serious and fraught. Harry never spoke to John Boyd again, and would not go to their home on any occasion, though Helen and Dudu remained close. Their only other family, social contact was Helen's cousin, Margaret, and her husband, Peter and their two daughters, one of whom was Peggy's age exactly.

The Kalpakians moved to a small house that seemed palatial after the two-room cottage, and soon after that they moved into an apartment behind a grocery store, the first of several small grocery stores he either rented or bought. The girls slept on bedding tossed over orange crates. Harry

Kalpakian was shrewd and frugal and in 1931, the year that they became American citizens, they bought a house—cash—and a new Pontiac. Later he bought another grocery store where he rented space out to an Italian butcher who, my mother remembers happily, played an accordion when there weren't a lot of customers. Harry Kalpakian only took vacations between changing grocery stores. These were all modest shops, literally mom-and-pop affairs. Helen worked by his side, while at home Angagh looked after the younger girls. My mom remembers as a high school student riding the bus to her father's grocery store and stocking the shelves every Thursday after school for which her father paid her the going rate, twenty-five cents an hour. Despite the Depression, the Kalpakian daughters had a sunny, much-loved, happy childhood, experiences my mother has chronicled in her *Centennial Memoir* (2019).

The daughters grew up Methodist simply because from their Haas Avenue house they could walk to the nearby Methodist church. No Apostolic incense and incantation for the Kalpakians. They attended St. James Armenian Apostolic church only for special occasions. And yet, Helen and Harry each remembered St. James Armenian Apostolic church generously in their wills. Helen Kalpakian's funeral in 1987 was presided over by an Armenian Apostolic priest and as he incanted prayers at her graveside, none of us present could understand a word he said other than Amen.

Of the four Kalpakian daughters, Betty and Harriet (born 1935) were American citizens by birth; Angagh, and Pakradouhi both applied for and got their own citizenship papers in 1941. At this time Pakradouhi officially changed her name to Peggy, the nickname given to her by her Boyd cousins who were teenagers. They couldn't pronounce her old country moniker; Peggy probably was taken from Baby Peggy, a well-known child star of the silent films. When Pakradouhi enrolled in kindergarten, she was already Peggy Kalpakian. All these girls excelled in school, earning scholastic and city-wide honors. Two went to University of Southern California, two to UCLA. Harry and Helen Kalpakian achieved their dreams, *assimilate, assimilate*, and paid for these achievements not only with unremitting work, but I suspect with the goods left undeclared, the diamond rings and brooches, the gold bracelets; perhaps they found that bribery, such an accepted mode of exchange in the old country, also worked well in the new country. Never mind what he'd sworn to Mr. Brumley, the vice-consul in Constantinople, in order to *assimilate, assimilate*, my grandfather sold some of the rugs they had brought.

But many of these rugs remained in the family and once lay across the hardwood floors of my grandparents' homes, and now in the homes of their grandchildren, five in my house alone. Two of them are here in the room where I write. Sometimes the sunlight falls at a certain angle across these old carpets, and their dull colors suddenly beam with richness, with brilliant red and blue, with flecks, seemingly, of gold. When this happens, they glow, and I wonder what hands created these rugs? How were these threads dyed and colored and what incredible skill must have gone into pulling them on to looms and pulling these intricate patterns out of nothing. In Constantinople a century ago they were rolled up, placed in the hold of a ship; they have crossed the Atlantic and Mediterranean and Aegean. They have lain on the floors of homes that have vanished under the wrecking ball. They have felt the feet of children who have long since grown up, of people who are long dead. They astonish me. And then the light moves and they go back to being dull and old and frayed at the edges, and I return to work.

VIII

The four Kalpakian girls married Protestants. The Kalpakian daughters all married non-Armenian men with Anglo names. Some of my cousins have blue eyes and fair hair. All the grandchildren were brought up in Southern California, where, certainly in that era, nearly everyone was from somewhere else, and the tract houses we all lived in comprised a sort of White Bread Eden. But other than the annual Armenian picnic where you might go with Grandma and get your cheek pinched, and be hugged by the old ladies who would chatter in Armenian with her, all of us grew up utterly unconnected to Armenian culture. Except for the food—which was part of any family occasion, great or small—we had not the language, not the religion, not the music or literature or culture or any of it. So assimilated are the children and grandchildren and great-grandchildren of Helen and Harry Kalpakian, so ignorant of all that pall of innuendo attached to being an Armenian, even a "starving Armenian," that when a college acquaintance once remarked to me, in a joking, offhand fashion (presumably referring to financial acumen) "It takes two Jews to beat an Armenian," I had no idea what he meant. No idea at all.

So I was very surprised when, as a nineteen-year old university student, I attended a class, or a tea at the home of a professor. (This was back in the day when professors felt obliged to host one such afternoon every term.) The class was over, and I was standing by the fireplace awaiting my ride. The professor and his wife had a foreign student boarding with them and he came home, into the livingroom, and spoke to me cordially, and I replied in kind. He was a nice enough young man, a graduate student in agronomy, well mannered with an odd accent. I asked where he was from. *Istanbul*, he replied. I said my mother had been born in Istanbul. *Ah*, said he, brightening, *are you Turkish? No*, I replied, *I am Armenian*, and instantly—like voltage applied to my hands and feet and temples—immediately I knew enough to loathe him, and to know that he despised me. No more was said.

What had so swiftly, so certainly transpired between us had to do with the Allied defeat at Gallipoli, with the building of the Berlin-Baghdad railway and the German and his horse; it had to do with Haigauz watching his father die of starvation and his mother stripped naked before she was killed; it had to do with Miss Towner offering my grandmother life-saving sanctuary at the Adana Girls' Seminary. It had to do with my grandfather being able to work in the German dry goods store rather than being conscripted to serve in the Turkish army. It had to do with Khatchadour Krakirian being released the very day he was to be hanged.

It had to do with leaving Adana in the middle of the night, pressed with bayonets onto a train heading to Syria, and with the *SS Bukovina* plying toward Constantinople, where my mother would be born. It had to do with this precious passport, now in my hands, stamped by the Turkish police, allowing the Kalpakians to leave the country where they had lived all their lives and yet remained foreign, where their own language could not be spoken, their religion could not be practiced in churches, where two thousand years of culture had to be shrouded. It had to do with carrying what you could not declare, not only literally—the rings and bracelets, the last few of which still clanked and rattled after my grandmother's death—but metaphorically, spiritually to carry always the burden of what you could never declare outright: the past.

It had to do with events so monstrous and cataclysmic they could not be altogether silenced, and if for my grandparents, their old country past existed only to be ignored, denied or repudiated, nonetheless it dripped down, the past did, silent as the intravenous bag beside the patient's bed, the bag itself out of sight, the fluid going directly into the vein. I have inherited things from the people in this passport photo, things besides their olive complexions, their dark eyes, dark hair, their facility for languages. Instinctively I define myself in opposition to what's around me, a foreigner's reflex, not a native's. I carry that indelible strain of sadness I sense in every other Armenian I have met, like an extra chromosome in the blood, that sadness, as though we somehow all have knowledge of events in which we did not participate. I keep secrets.

I kept secrets from my own children. As my sons grew up, did I share with them the Armenians' tragedies? No. Haigauz's story? No. I'm sure I told them the Cup of Coffee story! Did I tell them of the grandparents going third class, and deported to Piraeus, and their return? No. I told them the Hot Water Tap Story! I emphatically did not describe the massacres, the forced marches, the unburied bones bleaching in the desert that lay of the root of the Kalpakians leaving Turkey. These events seemed so far distant from bright American childhoods that to give them voice would somehow have cast a dreadful pall. Clearly, this is exactly what my grandparents thought with regard to their children and grandchildren. The irony is not lost on me. I perpetuated the silence.

When children leave home, the parents always gnash and thrash over what they have failed to do: what have they not stressed or taught? What dangers have they not made clear? My relationship to my Armenian past came into sharp, painful, personal focus in 2002 and involved another Turkish student like the one I had met when I was nineteen so many years before.

In 2002 I took my youngest son, Brendan, down to University of Southern California to be a freshman at the Flora L. Thornton School of Music where his brother was a senior. USC had given Brendan a room in the scholarship dorm, though he was not a scholarship student. (Bear was, and, I assumed, the scholarship dorm assignment for Brendan was a gift for the name McCreary.) We were getting him settled in the dorm room when I found out that Brendan had been assigned a Turkish roommate, a foreign student from Turkey. My heart knotted in my body and I suffered an immediate maelstrom of conflicting emotions. Might it be best to ask USC housing to move him to a different room? But what sort of message is that? Especially for someone just starting out in life? And even if USC complied, probably they wouldn't move him within the scholarship dorm, more likely to one of those dorms that had hard-partying reputations. And how could I convey to my eighteen-year old son why he ought to ask for a different assignment when I had told him so very little, almost nothing, of the family's past? How wise would it be to intervene, to evade, to opt out? Should I merely stay silent and hope for the best? But what if. . . ? Brendan didn't even have the background or history to understand what might possibly befall him with his Turkish roommate.

Before I left him that afternoon in his new room, his new life, I sat Brendan down and tried to make up for the secrets I had kept. I tried to explain the centuries of oppression under the Ottoman Empire, and the events of 1915 that had cost his great-grandmother the lives of her family, and had driven the Kalpakians to flee. I tried to explain calmly, but with enough background, passion, information—call it what you will—so that he would understand that though these events were ages ago, decades long past, they remained important, that he must be aware of them. I'm not sure he did understand. Certainly he thought it odd

that in the last few hours I had with him, I would telling him
this grisly tale of enmity going back four hundred years.

However, by the time I was done, I had developed a
plan. "So," I finished up, "here's what you do. You tell him
you are Italian."

"What?"

"You look Italian. When it comes up, you tell him your
family is Italian. You don't say you're Armenian."

"Why?"

"Didn't I just finish telling you why?" Falling back on
the old parental saw, I added, "Just do as I ask."

Thus, I asked my own son to deny his ethnicity, his
family, his Armenian identity. I perpetuated all the old declarations and denials. I was sick at heart, but not contrite;
I felt I had done, if not the right thing, at least enough to
protect my son.

The Turkish roommate arrived two weeks late. I never
met him. Brendan said he was a perfectly nice guy whose
English was not that great. When the subject came up—
and it did—Brendan said he was Scots/Irish on his father's
side, Italian on his mother's. The Turkish room-mate found
a lot Turkish friends at USC, and on Sunday afternoons,
Brendan would play soccer with the Turks. I would sit at
home, twelve hundred miles away, and worry that ninety
years was not enough time to keep my beloved son from
peril. I could not even call my mother and share my anxi-
eties; she would have been worried sick, undermining her
health when she already had so much else to worry about. (I

never did tell her. She did not know Brendan had a Turkish roommate till 2018 when she read this memoir in draft.)

The semester passed without incident. The following term, Brendan and a group of guys he met at the scholarship dorm, all moved to an apartment. The Turkish student returned to Turkey. But my telling Brendan to lie about his ethnicity sent him on a long quest for his own roots among the Armenian students at USC. These students were from a far more recent wave of immigration, in the 1990s, after the fall of the Soviet Union. They may have come from different diasporas, but they spoke Armenian; they were raised among Armenian ethnic traditions, Armenian culture, and in the Armenian church. Brendan was not. Their long-instilled animosities, their deep woe mixed with rage at Turkey's ongoing failure to acknowledge the Genocide, seemed to Brendan their dominant theme. On a less polemical note, there were things he recognized. He made one close Armenian friend, and when he went to this friend's parents' home, walked in the door, and caught the scent of Armenian cooking, tears came to his eyes. Sadly his friend had to leave LA and move to Toronto because of immigration troubles.

The Los Angeles that Harry and Helen Kalpakian arrived at in 1923 did not have a sprawling, lively community of Armenians maintaining traditions even in the diaspora. The Kalpakians had Armenian friends, of course, and the small core of my grandmother's family, her sister, her cousin, but for everyone in their generation, the mantra was *assimilate assimilate*. The deep woes, the bitter animosities that animated the twenty-first century Armenian students at USC would not have been articulated, certainly not dwelt upon. Harry and Helen Kalpakian cared less about maintaining who they were, and more about becoming who they might be, American citizens. And if their past died in an airless silence, they would have said, did basically say, what of it? Can the past be cherished if it is not preserved? Can it be preserved if it is not cherished? Can it be either, if no words are fastened to it for shape and texture? I would answer probably yes to those questions. I would say for my family, all my family, the living and the dead, the lost and the found, the near and the far, the past is like sand or lint or ash, something gritty and secret, caught in your clothes, in the seams and pockets, under your fingernails, in the cache-corsets of your mind, the undeclared regions of the heart, clinging there indelibly, no matter how much hot water you use to wash it off.

CHAPTER TWO

"BRIDE OF THE WAVES"

When all that was promised the Saints will be given
And none will molest them from dawn until ev'n
And the earth will appear as the Garden of Eden
And Jesus will say to all of Israel "Come home!"

> *~Mormon Hymn*
> *"Now Let Us Rejoice"*
> *William D. Phelps*

I

In Fremont County, Idaho times were hard, cash money was scarce, and families were large. People who lived there either farmed, or worked in the sugar beet fields that dotted the Snake River plateau, or toiled in the sugar beet factory that supported, indeed, that had created the town of Sugar City in 1904. Here, in September 1923 vivacious, voluble, energetic, Lila Johnson, eighteen years old wed Laurence Lutz. Lila's shy elder sister, Anetta, served as bridesmaid. My father, Bill Johnson, age five in 1923, probably attended the wedding of his aunt, along with his parents, Will and Mae. They and many others of the extended Johnson clan all lived nearby.

However, the groom's brother, Willie Lutz, was not present. Willie was still on a two year mission for the Latter-day Saints, proselytizing in New Zealand. Later that autumn, Willie did return from the mission field, and before he went home, he came to visit his brother Laurence who was farming in Hibbard, Idaho, not far from Sugar City. When Lila met Willie, she was certain he was the man for her sister, Anetta. Willie had a sweetheart back home; in fact, he was actually engaged to this girl. Lila knew this, but it didn't stop her from insisting that Anetta (who was still living with their mother) should come stay in Hibbard for a bit. Anetta had always lived in her sister's shadow (where she had lots of company; just about everyone who knew Lila lived in her shadow) and she obeyed.

I look at Willie and I have to smile, because I hope with all my heart that my sister is right and this is the man for me. God passed emery paper over Willie's face. He was so smooth and clean-shaven and chiseled-looking. Bright eyes that look right at you and a narrow mouth with a fine, firm smile. Willie played the cornet, played it just like an angel would have if angels played the cornet which I'm not sure they do. We spent many hours that week—was it only a week?—on my sister's front porch, talking for such a long time. I asked Willie all about the mission field in New Zealand, and he asked me all about me. I don't have much to tell, I said, there's nothing too interesting about me. But Willie said: You

*do yourself an injustice. I think you are one of the most
interesting persons I have ever met, and certainly the
most beautiful.*

Willie and Anetta fell so in love in that short, intense,
glorious moment that Willie went home, broke off his engagement, returned to Fremont County, and married Anetta
Johnson in December, 1923. They got a place in Sugar City
and Willie got a job in the sugar factory. Ten months later
they were parents. Two years later Willie was dead.

II

I learned this story and others in summer, 1977 when
I went to Ogden, Utah to research the novel that became
These Latter Days. This trip was one of the great journeys
of my life, not in the sense of exotic adventure, but because
of the richness, the downright treasure trove of lore and
photographs that my great-aunts, Lila and Anetta, gifted
to me, in those couple of days we visited with them. My
father and mother came with me on this trip, my mom to
help me take notes, my father to "break the ice," After all, I
had not seen his elderly Mormon relatives, or had any sort
of communication with them in more than a dozen years. I
wouldn't exactly know what to say. But my dad, a charming
outgoing man, put everyone at ease, and clearly, he adored
his aunts, Lila and Anetta, and they adored him as well.

Anetta's second husband had died in 1970, and she
now lived with her daughter who had gone on vacation.
Anetta, too fragile to be left alone, was staying with Lila
and Laurence in the interim. Frail Anetta and bustling Lila

were a study in contrasts. Lila at seventy-two was bright-eyed, capable, her white hair cut short and curled; she wore a neat housedress and an apron that looked to have been ironed. Anetta, at seventy-nine was physically immobile, thin, soft-spoken, and dementia had made serious inroads on her cognitive processes. To make polite conversation, I asked her, "Where do you live, Aunt Anetta?"

She replied in her thin, quavery voice, "I live uh. . .I live. . .uh. . . I live. . ." She looked perplexed and then she called out to Lila who was in the kitchen fixing dinner for eight people. "Lila! Lila! Where do I live?"

"You live with your daughter," Lila called back.

"I live with my daughter," Anetta said, clearly relieved.

So I was considerably shocked the following day when Lila and Anetta showed me a photograph of Anetta's first husband, Willie. He was quite beautiful with fine, chiseled features, and curly dark hair. Anetta said plainly, "Willie and I had thirty-four months together." Not nearly three years. She could not say where she lived, but she knew she had thirty-four months with him before he died, leaving Anetta with two small children. (And clearly, Anetta was pregnant for eighteen of those months and had an infant and a toddler to care for.) Anetta spoke of those thirty-four months not as though more than a half century separated her from Willie, nor even wistfully, as though Willie was someone she had long since consigned to memory, but as though she might delightedly turn to him, right now, in this room, and smile, and that he might smile back.

"He was so young," I said. "What did he die of?"

"Sugar on the lungs," Anetta replied "The doctor said, Mrs. Lutz, your husband has died of sugar on the lungs."

I thought I had misheard her. "Sugar on the lungs? What does that mean?"

She reiterated carefully, as though I were hopelessly stupid or deaf, "Sugar On The Lungs."

I feel fairly certain that "sugar on the lungs" is not an actual medical term, but in the 1920s it probably described a good many deaths for men who worked in the sugar beet factories of Idaho. In *Beet Sugar and the West*, Leonard Arrington tells how sugar beets, beginning in the 1890's with new technology and processes, proved lucrative for the Utah Sugar Company, as well as for the Mormon church which was deeply allied to it. Sugar City Idaho, where Willie and Anetta lived for those thirty-four months was the very definition of the company town. The Sugar City factory had opened in 1904, and by 1905, with typical Mormon industry and hard work, a town was solidly grounded with homes, a hotel, a Latter-day Saint church, a school being built. The Idaho Sugar Company factory and its rhythms—sounds and smells and cycles, shifts and whistles—dominated life in the surrounding area. Mr. Arrington's photographs show that as late as the 1930's the planting of sugar beet fields was done with horse-drawn plows. My dad, Bill Johnson worked in the sugar beet fields for thirty-five cents an hour as a teenager in the 1930s. However, unlike his father, his grandfather, and many of his uncles including Willie Lutz, Bill Johnson never labored in the sugar factory itself.

After Willie's death Anetta, impoverished, and with no husband to provide for her, and no skills to speak of, took her children, and moved back in with her widowed mother, Jeannettie Johnson. In his short, rambling account of his childhood and youth, my dad wrote, "I remember once we visited Grandma, and Aunt Anetta was there as she lived with Grandma with her two children. Her husband, Willie, (Laurence's brother) had a cornet. It was old and banged up, but with a case, and Aunt Anetta gave it to me. This was the greatest gift anyone could bestow on me. I was thrilled to say the least. I began to practice the cornet, just blowing it to make a noise."

And make a noise he did! Willie Lutz's tragic, early death would exert a tremendous, if oblique influence on the life of my father who was only eight in 1926. Learning to play that cornet would prove crucial to the man Bill Johnson became, and playing "Bride of the Waves" on that cornet in 1935 in Pocatello, Idaho would crown and confirm his commitment to a set of values that guided his life for ninety-four years.

III

Ironically, since the Johnsons as a tribe were patriarchy-loving Latter-day Saints, Lila Johnson Lutz (1905–1990) was the strongest and most vivid personality in her generation. I make this judgment via my father. Of the Johnson men, his uncles, George, Leslie, Sydney, and Howard, I knew nothing whatever; he never spoke of them. Of Stan and Jess, I knew a little. But Lila figured in so many anecdotes! High-spirited, certain of her own correctness, a devout Mormon, mother to seven children, caretaker of many others, farmer, genealogist, cook, canner, and keeper of the family lore, Lila Johnson Lutz was both charming and formidable (again, in the sense that the French use that word, a force to be reckoned with). Her stories were legion, and she delighted in the telling, and later, in writing them down. These written accounts listed her two sisters, Anetta and Minnie as co-authors, but the storytelling voice is clearly Lila's. Her tales, written or told, always reflect happily on her relatives, the protagonists. If you were listening to her speak (as I was, those few days in Ogden in 1977) you must laugh when the story is funny, let your eyes grow wide when it concerns some prodigious feat, nod when it is poignant, but please, do not ask stupid questions that will attempt to broaden that story beyond the narrative limits set by the teller, Lila, who bubbled over brightly with stories of the Johnsons outsmarting others! The Johnsons enjoying some miraculous piece of good luck! Enduring some terrible trial over which they (naturally) triumphed!

However, Lila's stories stepped tidily around inconvenient domestic arrangements as if they were cowpies in a meadow. For instance, her grandmother, Mary Johnson left Gustav Johnson in 1867 after four years of marriage and two little sons. In 1868 Mary married a Mr. Jensen, by whom she had many more children. I asked Aunt Lila how did Mary Johnson get a divorce in 1867 Utah Territory. In reply, and in a manner of speaking, I was told to pass the peas. I could not help but wonder, given Mary's marriage the following year, if Mr. Jensen might have been waiting in the wings, But I was not so crass (or stupid) as to actually suggest this. Mary's younger son by Gustav took the name Jensen. Only her older son, William Andrew, Lila's father, remained a Johnson. (The Johnson/Jensens had semiannual family reunions as late as the 1990s. Perhaps they still do.)

Gustav Johnson, born about 1840 in Stockholm, Sweden, had converted to the Saints there and emigrated. He married Mary in 1862 in Salt Lake. In 1867 Gustav either abandoned his wife, or was abandoned by her. Unclear. Certainly Lila never ventured anywhere near what miseries might have driven a Mormon couple to part ways in the 1860s. Gustav apparently went to California following their breakup. According to Lila: one day, decades later, her own father William A. Johnson Sr. *Just happened to be in California and recognized him!* (My italics and exclamation do not do justice to Lila's tone of voice.) *Well,* Lila went on, *all was instantly forgiven!* And William A. Sr. brought his father, Gustav, home to Idaho where William and his wife, Jeannettie tended him lovingly until his death.

After my gaffe with divorce, I knew better than to blunder into the obvious. All is forgiven? Really? On a street in California William A. Sr. recognized a man he hadn't seen since he was four? Really? He brought him home and his wife Jeannettie took in this old man? Looked after him till he died? Really? Genealogical tables I found later testified that Gustav actually died in Sacramento California in 1896. Did Lila know that? I'm sure she did. Did it matter? Probably not.

In Lila's eyes, and in her stories, her relatives are all brave and strong and clever; the men, especially, are pillars of wisdom, the women are pillars of strength. Everyone is devout. The evening in 1977 that we were her guests, she insisted that her father, William A. Senior (1863–1915) graduated from BYU and spoke Icelandic. (After we left Lila's house my father scoffed at this; he said that William A. Sr. was a drunk and that when he died, no one was sorry to see him go, not his widow, nor his five grown sons, nor the five underage children he left behind, one a mewling infant, a baby so frail she was not expected to live.) The family was probably financially ruined even before he died in November, 1915. Locusts had taken the crops the summer before. If it's true that William Andrew Sr. died in a hospital (as Lila said he did) there would have been ruinous medical bills as well.

Jeannettie Lance Johnson (1869–1937) had married him in 1886 when she was seventeen. She bore twelve children in twenty-eight years, the eldest, my grandfather, William A. Johnson Jr. born 1887 and the youngest, Elaine (the baby who did live) born in March 1915. Between Anetta (1898) and Lila (1905) there was a girl who died as a toddler. In addition to those eleven children Jeannettie lived a frontier life cooking, canning, farming, killing livestock, slopping hogs, keeping hens, healing the sick, trimming wicks, churning butter, heating water in iron kettles, washing, ironing, tending, mending, making soap, biscuits, knitting, running the Relief Society (the domain of Mormon women) and anything else you can imagine. Despite mastering these skills, when her husband died, she had no means sufficient to support a fatherless family. She and her dependent children, Lila, Anetta, Minnie, Howard and baby Elaine, moved among the homes of her five grown sons, Will, Sydney, Leslie, George and Jess who lived in or around Fremont County, Idaho. Eventually Jeannettie had her own place in American Falls, Idaho, which is where Anetta joined her after Willie's death in 1926. (I do not know how Jeannettie paid the rent, or if one or some of her sons rented it for her.) Jeannettie outlived her husband by twenty-two years, dying in 1937. She did not remarry. Easy to understand why.

According to Lila, Jeannettie's parents, Lewis and Temperance Lance, were just as outstanding and wonderful as the Johnsons! They started out in Texas and moved by team, to St. Louis for Lewis's health; he was blind. (And though I did not ask, "Really, blind?" Lila clarified, "Yes, blind.") Their many migrations, Lila described as "They decided to travel," as though they had packed their bags for a Caribbean cruise, and not that they continually piled their children, their invalids, their worldly goods, their harmoniums, their bureaus and family Bibles into wagons and yoked those wagons to oxen or mules or horses, and lumbered on uneven trails for days, weeks. Lila said Temperance and Lewis left Texas in 1865, moving on to Kansas in 1866 where Lewis contracted a disease known as "Milk Leg" which caused one leg to go pale and shrink. He was bedridden for over a year and Temperance supported the family by running a restaurant. They had another child there before traveling with a freight company to Utah. They arrived in Utah in 1868 where Lewis (without further explanation or ado) was cured of his blindness, the "Milk Leg" apparently cured by bed rest. Not until they came to Utah did they actually join the Latter-day Saints, husband and wife baptized in January 1869, the ice cut in the river so they could go under the waters of baptism. Total immersion. Temperance was pregnant with Jeannettie who was born June 28 1869.

The Lances left Utah and moved to Idaho, birthing and burying various children along the way. They moved around Utah and Idaho many times thereafter, including to Rockland, Idaho where they were the first white family to put down roots there, though roots is too strong a term, since they left there as well. But not before Lewis made peace with the Blackfoot chief who suffered from an eye ailment, and Lewis gave him some medicine that had helped when he was blinded. By 1881 the Indians were peaceful and there were enough Saints in Rockland to build a church. Still, bad luck seemed to dog Lewis Lance; he was one-handed after an accident in a molasses mill, but this did not stop him from pursuing the possibility of plural marriage. Lewis took his daughter Jeannettie, then a young teen, to meet the prospective plural wife. On the way home Jeannettie told him that the woman, "Didn't empty her thundermugs often enough, and her biscuits were hard and didn't have enough salt."

Lila pealed out laughter at this. "There was no more said of polygamy, and no plural marriage!"

Nineteenth century Idaho demanded of any who settled there, a life of unremitting labor beset by want, a crude

life where your best assets were good health, sheer physical strength, and stamina, a stout heart and a firm hand. I
seriously doubt that Lila's father William A. Senior, went to
BYU, or spoke Icelandic, but give him this: he homesteaded
in Idaho in the 1880's, dry-farming there. (Growing wheat
with no irrigation.) Four children were born in a dugout,
literally under the earth, the roof bolstered with timbers.
Later, William A Senior built the first brick kiln, and with
these bricks he built the first brick house in the county.
After that they used the dugout for a chicken coop (this
gives you some idea of its size). A photograph testifies to
the truth of the family's prosperity; they stand in front of
the two-story brick house which rises up, raw and proud
in an empty field. Lila's stories of her frontier childhood
on that Idaho dry farm are full of Biblical threats, fighting
plagues of locusts banging pans through the fields to scare
them away while the locusts flew into their hair and eyes
and mouths. They endured floods and harsh winters. They
endured, sustained by their Mormon faith.

For all the touting of Rugged Individualism in settling
the West, in fact, cooperation was essential for survival,
and in this the Mormons excelled. Communal cohesion
sustained the Latter-day Saints through many trials. They
were bedeviled (not perhaps the best word) from their
very beginnings, their founding in upstate New York, c.
1825 when God gave Joseph Smith golden tablets for him to
translate and record. According to this new gospel, in Biblical times there were dramatic clashes between the Nephites
(good guys) and the Lamanites (bad guys) here on the

North American continent, and after Jesus's resurrection, he came to North America and walked among these people. Thus, Mormonism was a truly new gospel, a religion that focused on the new world. Having translated these golden tablets, aided by angels, Smith declared himself a new apostle. Joseph Smith was from all accounts charismatic and convincing, and his new beliefs collected many converts. However many people thought Smith a charlatan and heaped hostility on the Saints, so much so, the new church felt compelled to leave New York State. Over some twenty-plus years they were forced ever westward in their search for a place in which to shelter and root their community, to practice their religion in peace. In each new place they settled they were met with opposition that escalated into violence. They were reviled sometimes for their religious practices like plural marriage, or larger controversies that beset ante-bellum America. (They took in runaway wives, but not runaway slaves.) Also, the Mormons were hard workers, and so communally connected that they voted as a bloc, and this gave them power that the locals would have resented. For nearly two decades they were burned out of every Eden they created. Smith himself was killed by a mob in the Carthage, Illinois jail while he awaited trial.

After strenuous in-fighting, Brigham Young took on the leader's mantle. Of Brother Brigham, one may safely say that he had not only the charisma of a leader, but the organizational skills of a born CEO as well. Brigham led the Mormons to Zion, what is now Utah, journeys of unimaginable hardship and travail. As the President of the Church he alone had the right to receive revelations from God, and God offered insights and instructions on how to move vast ragged chains of men, women, children, animals, wagons and goods across an unforgiving terrain. God's instructions were duly enshrined in the *Doctrine and Covenants*, a sacred text. In reading *Doctrine and Covenants*, one marvels at God's attention to detail, right down to how the handcarts shall be built. (Two wooden wheels each three or four feet in diameter, with thin iron tires. Wooden shafts about five feet long, connected with a cross-piece at the end.)

Any Mormon family with roots in the nineteenth century has heroic ancestors who took part in the Saints' struggles. According to Lila, the Johnsons had Mary Louise Allard, widowed with two little children who converted to the faith in Canada, and who was part of the famous Handcart Brigade who walked from Iowa to Zion.

In Coralville, Iowa, you can see this marker:

SOUTH OF THIS BOULDER ON THE BANKS OF
CLEAR CREEK IS THE SITE OF THE MORMON
BRIGADE CAMP. IN 1856 SOME THIRTEEN HUN-
DRED EUROPEAN IMMIGRANTS, CONVERTED
TO THE MORMON FAITH, DETRAINED AT IOWA
CITY, THE END OF THE RAILROAD. ENCAMPED
HERE THEY MADE HANDCARTS AND EQUIP-
MENT FOR THEIR JOURNEY ON FOOT TO SALT
LAKE CITY.

It's still possible to stand there and imagine the mill-
ing people, the animals, the smoke from the fires, and the

wailing infants (some of whom are buried there) as these faithful piled in their goods, their hopes and dreams into handcarts they had made themselves. The Saints set off, walking to Salt Lake, to pit their strength and faith and energies against the vast plains, against nature itself.

The Handcart Brigade exemplifies the highly organized nature of Mormon migrations: responsibility carefully tiered, obligations distinctly allotted. Ten Handcart Brigade companies made the trip from Iowa City to Salt Lake City between 1856 and 1860. Their three thousand names are listed in the definitive book, *Handcarts to Zion*. Mary Louise Allard does not appear anywhere in this book, nor does anyone with a name even vaguely like that. But even if Lila's stories are untrue, I must confess there have been times in my life when I've taken heart to think that I might have come from people who had such strength and courage, such grit that they walked from Iowa to Salt Lake.

Lila wrote these stories down, but her sister Minnie (who alone of the Johnson women had office experience) typed them up. Copied, and stapled, they were mailed out to the many Johnsons, including my father and his forty-odd first cousins. In reading these stories collectively what rises up from the page? Dust. You can all but taste the dust in the wake of wagons and oxen and horses as these restless people moved all over the Inter-mountain West. One story says William A. Sr., having got the wagons loaded and the oxen hitched to go to California, and the family all clambered up and ready to roll, changed his mind. Then and there. The writer in me longs to ask: *Did they just move back into the old place? Had they sold it? What did they do? What happened next?* But Lila, Anetta and Minnie in their telling of the incident were satisfied with "changed his mind," and that was the end of the story, Thank You Very Much.

In any event I find their itinerant life astonishing. After all the backbreaking and heartbreaking labor, literally plowed into the earth, to pack up their belongings and move again and again at the behest of. . . what? Bad luck? Fear? Failure? Locusts? Drought? Or some deep-seated reflexive American restlessness leavened with the hope that the next place would prove better? Aunt Lila's stories—in the best oral tradition since humans squatted in caves—relay the wanderings, the tribulations of these tribes with their wagons and women and children, and animals, people who were restless and rootless. They traveled in family packs, leaving graves, and cast off harmoniums along the way. They followed one another like Faulkner's Snopes clan; in nearly all their wanderings they went to join some other family member already living there, wherever "there" was.

But these devout Mormons were connected to more than the living. The Saints practice temple rites in which families are assured and endowed and sealed unto their wives and husbands and parents and children for time and all eternity (a fine phrase that rings throughout Mormonism). Thus they are guaranteed to be together in the Celestial Kingdom after death. So staunch was Lila Lutz's faith that in 1990 after Laurence's death, when her own health began to fail, she quit eating, certain, even eager to be reunited with him in the Celestial Kingdom.

The Mormons' Celestial Kingdom takes the Bible's "many mansions" literally. In the Celestial Kingdom Mormons can have many mansions, and the men can have many wives and hold great tracts of opulent celestial real estate. No matter how hardscrabble your life on earth, no matter how hungry or dirty or desperate or driven you were on earth, no matter if you ate nothing but mush and spent your working life shackled to a plow, looking at the butts of horses or mules or oxen, if your fields and house and hair swarmed with locusts, if you labored in a sugar factory and died of the sugar on the lungs, you were entitled to a gorgeous afterlife in what amounted to a really nice neighborhood. If all these Johnsons and Lances and Lutzes and all their kin truly believed they would rejoice together amid all that fine real estate in the Celestial Kingdom, then perhaps all those many graves scattered across the West mattered less to them than the convictions of time and all eternity. I guess they're all reunited now, good Mormons, lolling in the land of milk and honey, but from everything I know of them, they would have got up and moved on from that too.

IV

In a family this sprawling, this numerous, there must surely have been a few people who were not exemplary or heroic, people with whom, perhaps, Lila might have quarreled. Oh wait, she never quarreled. She was always right. However, since Lila was the keeper of the family flame, there were bound to be those who drifted into oblivion. Such was the fate of the Hendersons, the family of my grandmother Mae Henderson Johnson. The Hendersons, Mormon converts from England, also lived in Fremont County, in fact, their youngest son was born in St. Anthony in 1912, the same place my father was born in 1918. But the Hendersons never figured in Lila's stories, and except for Mae and her sister Eva, their very names were lost to us.

A trunk they brought from England and a single photograph in my possession, that's all I have of them. The trunk must somehow have been given to my father because it has followed me in my various homes since 1974. The photograph was given to me by Eva Henderson Farnsworth, my grandmother's younger sister. We saw Eva on that 1977 trip as well, but separately from the Johnsons. Widowed, nearly eighty, and quite frail, Eva was nonetheless warm and welcoming. She generously shared her past, including fleeing her abusive first husband, Charles Bryant, a harrowing tale of Eva and her little son making their escape on a train to Arizona. She later divorced Bryant and married Ernest Farnsworth.

The photograph that Eva gave me clearly commemorates the Hendersons' departure from England in 1908 when Eva was about ten. They all look primly Edwardian, with a strong family resemblance. The oldest boy, sixteen year old Archie, looks eager, confident; the youngest boy looks bratty. The three girls—my grandmother Mae, her little sister Eva, and an older sister, Amy—look resigned, possibly a little afraid. The parents' expressions exude a sort of smug resolve.

William Ernest Henderson and his wife, Norah were both born in the early 1870's in England (he in Sussex, she in Hertfordshire). But they married—perhaps even met and married—in Scranton, Pennsylvania in 1891! Why, how, when did they go to Scranton? What did they do there? Their first child (the boy, Archie, who looks so confident in the photograph) was born in Scranton in 1892. They were back in Hertfordshire, England when a second child was born in 1893, and six more children born in England followed. I know all this from the Latter-day Saints genealogical charts so carefully annotated in my grandfather's elegant hand. But these gridded charts offer *nada*, not so much as a stick or spar for conjecture as to what might have brought them to Scranton in the first place. What made them leave Scranton? Why return to England? The very *fact* of Scranton on these charts, however, testifies that the Hendersons too were part of that restless cohort, people willing—for whatever reason, choice or necessity—to uproot, to move on, to move out into the unknown. In short, the discontents. Contented people do not leave. When the Hendersons came to America this time, c. 1908, as LDS converts, they stayed. What or who brought them to the wilds of Fremont County and St. Anthony Idaho, I have no idea, but everyone in this photograph lived and died in the West.

Lila had barely veiled disdain for her sister-in-law, Mae Henderson. When I visited in 1977 Lila gave me a studio photograph of her brother, Will and a be-spectacled, bookish-looking girl named Irene. Lila said her brother had been engaged to Irene. Why else would a young couple in that era have a studio photograph? Then, according to Lila, along comes Mae Henderson, pretty, plump, pink, and English, and Mae told someone she was going to "get" Will Johnson. Lila broadly implied that in doing so, Mae tricked Will into marrying her, probably with ploy of having yielded up the Final Favor with the risk of pregnancy. Will and Mae married in December 1914, a temple wedding, reserved for the only the most devout.

However, my father, Bill, their eldest, was not born until March 1, 1918, over three years after their marriage. A long lapse for a devout Mormon couple. Mormons believe that, just as there is an afterlife in the Celestial Kingdom, there is a Pre-Existence where unborn spirits cavort (or something) awaiting bodies and eager for the chance to be tested on earth so they can get to the Celestial Kingdom after death. These little spirits would, naturally, prefer Latter-day Saints parents, thus the incentive to large families. Perhaps Mae suffered miscarriages in those early years of her marriage. I have no idea. I did not know her well, and certainly would never have asked such an intimate question. I doubt my dad knew or ever asked, and probably never cared. Mae and Will Johnson had five more children, three girls, Evelyn, Leila and Elaine, born at two year intervals, and Frank, born 1926, all of them in St. Anthony, Fremont County, Idaho. A decade later another son, born in Coeur d'Alene, died in infancy.

Alone of his siblings, my dad most strongly resembles the Hendersons, the round face, broad forehead, big green eyes and full mouth of his mother, features he bequeathed to me (other than the green eyes). Mae must have been quite attractive as a young person, but by the time I met her, she was a stout, slow, pale woman with an unchanging, incurious, unruffled expression. She reminded me of a vanilla cupcake. I never once saw her moved beyond a shallow delta of blandness, never heard her laugh beyond a quiet titter, nor evince shock or joy beyond "Oh my," although I must say she was dazzling with a pair of knitting needles. She could watch TV and knit a whole blanket without so much as looking down. Also, she could read tea leaves. Her favorite phrase, indeed her favorite topic of conversation was who among her children or her various husbands "treats me like a queen."

One may safely say Will Johnson did not treat her like a queen. She led a life of poverty and hardship with him. Will died unexpectedly in January 1956 in Ogden, Utah. Mae remarried within two years, first to the dour Mr. Hoult (who, she assured us, "treats me like a queen") and shortly after he died, to a pleasant old gent, Mr. Dallof, who also treated her like a queen, and was rather nice to us into the bargain. When Mr. Dallof died, he left her with a house and some morsel of financial stability. She would have married again in the 1980s, but her sons, Bill and Frank, forbade it. Bill and Frank pointed out that her little house and her little income would not support two, and that the would-be groom was an eighty-five-old bounder.

V

When Bill Johnson was himself an octogenarian, he scrawled out "My Life." It rambles, often non-sequitur, glancingly tangential, describing his childhood till his early twenties. "My Life" does not ripple with gentle, happy-hued nostalgia. On the contrary, Bill describes the poverty, the over-crowding, the lack of heat, the outhouses. Much, most of what he wrote was something of a surprise to us (that is, to my mom and to me) because other than the occasional joking reference to Sugar City, my father almost never spoke of his childhood and youth.

We had never guessed at the truth of my dad's impoverished rural roots until 1961 when he, perhaps inadvertently, brought it to our attention. Following Will Johnson's death in 1956, some convolute cocktail of loyalty, guilt, obligation, even love, impelled my father every summer to use his two week vacation to drive to Utah to see his mother because "she was going to die." (She lived till 1989.) Every summer we piled into the Ford stationwagon, the tent strapped atop, the car loaded unto groaning. Bill drove the whole way, his left arm resting on the open window, a deeply tanned streak from his T-shirt sleeve to his wrist, the badge of the 1950s and 1960s paterfamilias. We always left before dawn to escape some of the worst of the heat, but it hardly mattered, not when you're going east into Nevada, and then north to St. George, Utah, and on to the greater Ogden area where many of my father's relatives now clustered.

But in 1961, on our way further north and east, to Yellowstone, we drove to Sugar City. My father, a cheerful man, lively, who loved to joke, to make funny faces, grew strangely quiet as we drove through Sugar City. The one main street remained much as it had looked when he had lived there, a nondescript, somnolent, row of mute Edward Hopperish buildings, no one stirring on the street. He stopped in front of a building that was once a bank, and said he remembered his teacher sitting on the steps crying her eyes out when she learned that all her savings had vanished the day the bank failed in 1929. So quiet was the sidewalk, the whole town, that I could picture her, a young woman with hands over her face. I could all but hear her sobs.

Bill drove around till he found some shells of buildings where he had once lived, two roofless stone huts, side by side, built by his Uncle Jess, one for Jess Johnson's family and one for Will Johnson's family. My dad stopped the car there, and we got out and walked around these overgrown, abandoned, squat hovels. I was a teen, old enough to assess what they testified to: no provision for heat or sanitation or running water, the tiny space for Will Johnson's family that sheltered seven people. Squalor and deprivation were everywhere apparent even among the weeds. In "My Life" Bill wrote of that 1961 trip, "We drove to row of houses where I had lived as a kid. No doubt our kids do not remember that, but I do. Maybe Peg doesn't remember either."

But my mom and I remember very well. At the time she and I exchanged glances, but said nothing.

Before they lived in that particular hovel, there were others. My dad remembered one house where his Uncle Les, his wife, and their two kids, his grandmother Jeannettie with her children Minnie, Howard, and Elaine, Bill and his siblings and his parents all lived together. When Bill first started school he and others rode by wagon from rural St. Anthony into Sugar City, the wagon pulled by two horses, and in the winter these horses were hitched to a sleigh, and heated bricks put in under the children's feet. Seventy years later, he still remembered the cold.

Much of my dad's "My Life" is taken up with boyish trouble. Trouble gotten into. Trouble evaded. His many cousins who lived nearby were either inspiration or co-conspirators.

Les and his family were going to move out into a nearby place, but before they did a group of us were in this empty house, and it was suggested that everyone in the group would shit on the floor. There were enough bodies around that each room was a shit pile. I guess we used newspaper for tissue or maybe we just pulled up our pants and waited till we had to shit again, and then returned to the empty house. Les's wife, Amy, was swearing to everyone that the floors were covered with kid shit. Fortunately no one ever found out which ones had done it, fortunate or my ass would have been mud. This episode occurred before Frank was born so I must have been five or six, old enough to shit someplace other than the outhouse. We must have lived there quite some

*time as all the kids in our family were born at home in
St. Anthony.*

Bill and a Henderson cousin, Chuck (Eva's son) built
a fire in an old barn to cook some potatoes, and by and by
old, dry manure in the barn smoldered, lit up, blazed, and
then lit up the barn and lit up the sky. Everyone came out
of the house to watch the barn burn. Mercifully it was some
distance from the house. When his father came home Bill
naturally used the age-old kid defense. "I tried to explain
it was Chuck's idea. . ."

Probably a lot of boy cousins took part in the summer
afternoons when a bunch of bare-assed boys would swim
at Bare Hole in a creek near the railroad tracks. When the
train whistle sounded, they would jump up out of the water
and wave wildly at the passing cars, laughing, and then dive
back into the creek.

Such antics, such high spirits were overshadowed by
want, if not outright misery, living in a series of dilapidated
rented shelters like the one we saw in 1961.

*I lived through the Depression in Sugar. I was always
glad when summer came and I went barefoot all summer. We moved from place to place, No indoor plumbing,
one water faucet, no heat except the cooking stove, a
4-burner coal or wood stove, no hot water, no bathroom,
two bedrooms. An electric cord hung down from one
room ceiling for light. We had an outdoor privy -- 2
holes. In the winter your ass would freeze and in the
summer, well between the manure of the barn and the
privy, it was disaster. I don't recall how we bathed, prob-*

ably didn't. The house had two bedrooms and another
room which was the kitchen, I guess you would say. Plus
a porch my dad enclosed with canvas from the sugar
factory. I slept in the porch. I haven't thought about this
since maybe 1930. In the same row of houses there was
a young man who was going to Ricks College. Wow, I re-
ally respected him. I thought someday I'll go to college."

In 1926—the same year that Anetta's husband Willie died of sugar on the lungs—my father's family moved from rural St. Anthony into Sugar City proper. Bill writes, "My Dad worked at the sugar factory in the fall. He took care of five to six big vats the size of our house, where I guess the sugar boiled (?) Or something. I guess he had to make enough money while the sugar factory was in full swing to hold him till spring, then he would paint houses."

Of his early teens Bill wrote, "I was never in trouble as a teenager. I worked hard and long. I never took anything that didn't belong to me and swearing was unthinkable, most likely because I played the cornet somewhat" [Unclear to me the connection he had in mind between swearing and playing the cornet!] He goes on, "I was responsible for sawing the wood for the stove on a daily basis. I had a probably 6-foot saw that was really hard work. I must have been about fourteen or fifteen. I did this after I delivered my Salt Lake Tribune papers around town. I recall once the newspaper offered a prize for so many new subscriptions. One prize I won was a box of cherry chocolates, one pound, and I gave it to my mother. No doubt it was the first chocolates she ever received."

In these Depression years, cash was hard to come by, and often Will Johnson took busted-up cars in trade for carpentry, or house painting. He would fix them up, drive them, or maybe trade them for some other sorts of goods or services. The most memorable of these cars was a Willys Overland that looked like a Model T. For fun Bill would sit behind the steering wheel and pretend to be driving, shift and brake and turn the wheel. (Good practice for a man who, as a pharmaceutical salesman covered a vast territory in Southern California and spent long hours in the car.) At some point Bill amused himself punching holes in the Willys Overland's radiator with a screw driver. "My Dad wasn't home and afterwards I had wished I were not home."

Bill was fond of an old saying "What won't fatten will fill," an expression that would always make my mom roll her eyes. But in his youth and childhood the phrase had meaning. She would also roll her eyes when (to the screeching delight of my sons) he would tell the story of helping out his father doing some carpentry for a family who invited them to stay for lunch. Bill's bowl of soup had a fly in it, and he ate around it. The fly neither fattened nor filled. For the most part the family monotonously ate mush. Cornmeal mush? Oatmeal? Barley? "We were so poor even the mice lived better because they stole the mush. . . As long as we had mush and milk and bread, who cared?"

The milk came from a cow they had for a while, "a Guernsey, a good source of milk," he wrote. "It was my job to milk night and morning. Maybe I was in the 6th or 7th grade. Anyway, how we lived through that, I'll never know. Never washed the udder and if shit fell in the bucket I'd just reach in with my hand and scoop it out. If there was any staph or ecoli, I scooped it out, most of it, I would say. . . no such thing as pasteurizing. We drank raw milk. How come we're all alive?" The cow later died "from eating sulphur block," and they dragged the carcass down to a creek bed and left it. They kept rabbits, a dog, a horse, a pig and at one time three goats. "One of pigs was wounded somehow. I think we ate him, not sure. Maybe he just died."

In such a life their relationship to animals was certainly not that of doting pet owners, but simple necessity, often replete with casual animal cruelty. In a ten-by-ten corral the Johnsons had a difficult horse that would bite anyone who tried to bridle him. Will Johnson intended to remedy this. Bill accompanied his father out to the corral and held the bridle and when the horse came at him, Will hit the horse, "over the head with a wide strap with all his might and almost laid him low. The horse raised up on his hind feet to kill my dad, front feet clawing," and at that Will struck him again, even more severely. "Then my dad ordered me on the horse, and opened the gate and away I went, at full speed." That horse never gave them any more trouble.

Also that summer of 1926, Bill, at eight years old, left home to live with Lila and Laurence on their farm in nearby Hibbard. This too reflected a frontier tradition of farming out children to work from an early age: one less mouth for the family, and one more pair of hands for the farmer, even if those were child's hands. As a child and moving into his teen years, every summer Bill helped Laurence milk his cows and take the milk to market, loading heavy ten- gallon milk cans on to a horse-drawn wagon and later onto a truck. He also farmed with Laurence. "When I was ten or eleven, I used to hitch Laurence's team up and go to the field and rake over where Laurence had plowed. Anyway the team was not moving very fast and I didn't have a whip, so once I stopped the team and held the horses and kicked them and then went back to work. At the end of the day I returned the team (Maude and Sailor) and went home. I had acres to do. I guess I got it all done."

At some point he must have been living year round with the Lutzes. He and their eldest boy, Elroy, one winter tied a rope around the horse, Chub, and the other end on the sleigh. "I rode Chub down the road. On the way back I galloped and the sleigh hit a post and Elroy went head over heels, not so to speak, but literally." Bill took the rope off Chub, somehow got his wounded cousin into the sleigh and pulled him home himself. Nearly seventy years later, he remembered, "Lila was furious, more than furious. I looked up furious in Webster's but it didn't give any synonyms worse than furious." Laurence and Lila took Elroy to Rexburg, the nearest doctor, perhaps twenty miles away, leaving the contrite Bill in charge of their four other children. When they returned Elroy's broken leg was in a cast. "Lila didn't send me home because the distance must have been ten or twenty miles, maybe more."

Bill often said that Lila saved his life, and he meant it literally, that she fed him, kept him from starvation. His deep, filial affection for the Lutzes formed in these early years, and persisted all his life without blemish. This is odd because my father and all his family put their relationships into shifting categories that can only be called Shit or Honey. People moved in and out of these categories, sometimes at the behest of actual circumstances, definite quarrels, and sometimes. . . well who knew why? All his relatives were, at one time or another, Shit or Honey. Only his brother Frank, Lila, Laurence, and Anetta remained steadfastly Honey. They could do no wrong.

VI

For most of my life everything my father said about Will Johnson kept him in the Honey category. Tone as much as content suggested that Will Johnson had an immense nobility of spirit. While I was growing up, while I was a young adult, in fact, the portrait of my grandfather that emerged, conjured from my dad's descriptions, implied that though fortune had not smiled on Will Johnson, poverty could not dim his moral grandeur. He was a fine, a talented man, able, devout, respected, educated, accomplished, a musician, an artist. Bill wrote in "My Life:" "In Sugar City our house was without carpet or linoleum. My dad measured out lines on the kitchen floor crisscrossing at perhaps a foot sized blocks. He proceeded to paint the squares in two different colors of paint. After the paint dried we were not without a pseudo-linoleum in the kitchen. When he was done, success measured in pride."

The Church of Jesus Christ of Latter-day Saints, its teachings, rituals and obligations formed the core of my grandfather's very being, foundational to the way he saw and moved through the world as a practicing Mormon. The good Mormon does not simply observe the Sabbath; he lives his faith, and the truly devout practice rites and rituals in sacrosanct places reserved for them. In addition to his monumental Great Timetable reconciling biblical, Mormon and secular history, Will Johnson did temple work, researching genealogy, creating volumes of pedigree charts, and family records. These are used for baptism for the dead, rites that take place in the temple, and in which only the most pious may participate. Will and Mae had been married in the temple, an honor reserved for the truly deserving and devout. Will acted as choir director, and leader of the Sunday School and youth groups. He held an exalted priesthood. (Only men can hold the priesthood. All the Mormon clergy, the whole hierarchy, are unpaid positions, most held by men.) Given Will's deep, firm commitment to the faith, I can only surmise that the Mormon church, its teachings and functions would have been essential to Bill Johnson's young life. And yet, "My Life" makes no mention whatever of the church, or anything associated with it. I find this strange.

In 1963 Mae Hoult (her second husband's name) mailed Bill three documents that were surprising to me when I found them after our basement flooded. The first is his baptismal certificate. (The Saints baptize at about age twelve.) On May 3, 1930 Bill was baptized by his own father. No few decorous drops on the forehead. Oh no. You wade into whatever body of water is designated holy (and in a rural Fremont, County, it was probably a stream or a pond) and the Elder puts his arm round your back, and says some grave, important words, and then, whoosh! Back you go, under the waters of baptism! Total immersion, coming up clean, sanctified, having taken your first step toward the Celestial Kingdom in the afterlife.

Two other certificates of ordination conferred upon Bill the priesthood. The first, the Holy Aaronic Priesthood, dated January 15, 1933 can be likened to a Jewish boy's bar mitzvah, effectively moving the boy into manhood. Two years later, age seventeen, March 10, 1935, Bill earned the Certificate of Ordination to the Holy Priesthood. The teenage boy was now a priest, an Elder in the Mormon church (as well as the eldest son of an esteemed Elder). I do not doubt for one moment that Bill fulfilled what the church and the priesthood—and his father—expected of him. Will Johnson, remember, was the man who in one emphatic session with a strap, cured an angry horse of the urge to bite. And yet no mention of the church intrudes upon Bill's casual narrative, and I never once heard him talk about the role of religion in his early life other than the vast admiration he had for his father.

So I was truly surprised, when, as he aged, my dad's estimation of his parents began to change, evolve. Mae, of whom he seldom spoke, occupied a new place in his thoughts. He began to refer to her often, to describe with sympathy and affection, even remorse. "My poor mother. . ." he would frequently comment, preface to regretfully recalling her hard, thankless life as the wife of Will Johnson, the rigors she'd endured bringing up a family in pioneer conditions, the washing done by hand in a washtub, the grim diet, the dirt and disease and hardship in hovels heated by a single woodstove, and lit only by candles or lanterns, or at best, a single bulb. In his late eighties Bill's pity for his mother deepened, and the admiration in which he had always held Will underwent a dramatic shift, beginning with offhand bitter remarks, and then, as dementia began to seriously erode his faculties, gathering anger and momentum.

Will Johnson could beget children, he could screw, but he couldn't support his family. His kids were hungry, but my dad still gave ten percent tithing of his lousy earnings to the sonofabitching church. The three girls all married young just to get away from him. (There's no way of knowing if that was true; the sisters did marry young.) *My parents farmed out both their sons so they wouldn't have to feed them.* (This was certainly true; they farmed Bill out to Laurence and Lila; they sent teenage Frank to live with Bill when he was a college student at Utah State, and could barely feed himself. He had to study, to hold a job, and keep hellion Frank in high school.) *There was nothing to eat. No heat except from a cookstove. We wiped our butts with the Sears catalogue or newspapers, or not at all. Not so much as a toothbrush.* (Bill never went to a dentist till he joined the navy; he had false teeth after that.) No Christmas presents. *No one ever had a birthday party. They forgot my tenth birthday altogether.*

After a stroke in 2005 Bill's unresolved rage against his father intensified. He would wobble around the house with his cane, find pictures of his parents, and deface them with magic markers. My mother and I hid the pictures of Will and Mae, moving them finally to my house. He would fill up page after page of yellow legal pads, illegible rambling, angry references to incidents that had (for us) no context, and laced with words like *vomit* and *shit*. What were these long-suppressed wrongs? We had no way of knowing. Over and over he scrawled insistently, *My Name is Bill, not William*. When I took him to the doctor, I alerted the staff that he must always be called Bill, never William; if anyone called him William, he would fly into a tirade, and demand to be taken out of there.

Slowly Bill's furious anger ebbed, and in his final few years, his parents seemed to fade from his mind altogether. Perhaps this was dementia's backhanded gift. His aunts, Lila and Anetta, his uncle Laurence, his brother Frank remained available to him, even vivid, but Will and Mae seemed to have crumbled like ashes, dispersed altogether in the dry winds desiccating memory.

VII

However pervasive the Saints' teachings, however powerful his father's influence, when I look at Bill Johnson's life it's clear to me that the core tenets that he lived by came not from the church, but from his relationship to that "old and banged up" cornet that Anetta gave him. In learning to play the cornet the man unfolds from the boy's experience. Once Willie's cornet comes into "My Life" that rambling, occasionally incoherent narrative gains focus, clarity and momentum, even enthusiasm. With that instrument Bill Johnson first put into practice the ideals of perseverance and strength that characterized the rest of his life. He be-lieved—and he raised his four children and two grandsons to believe— that if you donated your brains, your time, your unrelenting effort toward a goal, you could bring your dreams to fruition. In this quest you could not be lazy nor cheat nor skimp, but move forward bravely, no matter what obstacles lay in your way.

The cornet, "the greatest gift anyone could bestow on me," focused his energies. "I never had a lesson in my life, but would practice for hours just running the scales. No doubt the neighbors wished I had been given a harmonica instead, however I kept blowing. I took the attitude, if I practiced enough, I didn't need lessons." There would not have been any money for lessons in any event, and though his father played the violin (self taught as far as anyone knows) and worked constantly with church choirs, Will seems not to have given any thought or encouragement to Bill's cornet, except for one incident. "In the 7th or 8th grade I was playing marbles after school and I put the horn and the case down behind the back wheel of a teacher's car. That person moved the car and whambo! I had a flat cornet. I was sick at heart. When I got home my dad took a handle from a broom and hammered it through the horn bell so I could blow it. Oddly enough, he made only one crack in the horn just past the bell. But it worked. So I kept blowing."

Bill signed up for band in the eighth and ninth grade. "Music was furnished by the school, and by now I could read notes and knew the fingering. I was considered pretty good, and yet, no lessons to help me or give me more incentive." He mentions his band teachers by name, especially a Mr. Christianson. "He was my ideal. He played the trumpet better than anyone in the world. I remember that once I told him, 'Someday I will be better than you.'"

That spring students tried out to represent the school at the state competition that would be held in Pocatello, Idaho. Bill spent hours practicing "Bride of the Waves," a classic cornet solo by Herbert L. Clarke (1867—1945). Clarke played in the John Phillips Sousa band, and wrote many of the classic cornet pieces in suites, like "Sounds of the Hudson." Clarke also arranged another difficult classic for the cornet, "Carnival of Venice" that Bill played as well. These pieces are not by any means jazz, or even jazzy; they reflect the repertoire of an earlier generation, in fact, of Willie Lutz's generation, the early 1900's. Songs like "The Last Rose of Summer," "Believe Me If All Those Young Endearing Charms" tested technical virtuosity, not improvisation. "Bride of the Waves," (1904) required long passages of very difficult double-and triple-tonguing technique.

"We had tryouts at school and two or three of us, the winners, played our solos at a church meeting. The people who handled the program brought someone from Ricks College to be the judge." Bill and one other boy were chosen to go to State finals in Pocatello. The other boy, Bill notes, had had lessons for years.

Pocatello was the first city Bill Johnson had ever seen. "It was like going to Europe," he remembered. In the 1930s Pocatello had broad avenues with street lights; it had prosperous neighborhoods, and the city could boast some sixteen thousand souls. The students who came to Pocatello to compete were housed with local residents, probably the homes of well-to-do, civic-minded families, perhaps a school administrator, or a school board member who lived in one of those fine old, solid homes of the early 1900s. I imagine Bill Johnson carrying his cornet in a flour sack (the case was gone after the car rolled over it) walking up the porch steps, knocking, greeted by a portly, well-fed, cheerful Mormon matron. She led him through the front hall, past a parlor, possibly with one of those big radios in a wooden cabinet, past a dining room with oak furniture and lace curtains at the windows, up the stairs, showing him the bathroom with its indoor plumbing, opening the door to the room where he would sleep, and flipping on the electric light. When she closed the door behind him, I cannot begin to imagine what this boy thought: at home he slept on a porch enclosed with canvas stiffened with run-off from the sugar factory. At the table of these Pocatello worthies Bill Johnson first tasted marmalade. A revelation! Even in old age, his mind gnawed to tatters by dementia, we could still make him smile with orange marmalade.

Of the competition itself Bill wrote, "The judge asked me to replay the triple-tonguing of this piece, no piano accompaniment. I just stood up in front of this room and played." I can so vividly picture this room! Full of hopeful high school kids from all over Idaho, their hair slicked down, their fingers twitching with anxiety, their teachers, saying nothing, but frowning to listen to the competition. A bespectacled matron, her hands poised over the piano, drops them to her side. A judge, with thick, clean-shaven jowls, and a waistcoat over his paunch, asks the skinny boy with the cracked cornet to replay that especially difficult passage of "Bride of the Waves." Of his performance Bill wrote, "With the old cornet with a hole in the horn half way from the bell to where it makes its bend, I had to compensate for the tone."

At the end, the judges deemed Bill Johnson and "Bride of the Waves" the winner! The kid from Sugar City won the state competition! Imagine the applause! Bill Johnson was the best trumpet player in the whole state of Idaho! Holding Willie's battered cornet, he reveled in this moment of glory. I think this was perhaps the happiest day of his whole life. Validation of his hard work, his dedication, his unstinting application, indeed, the realization of his dearest ambition. Maybe he was even better than Mr. Christianson.

"My Life" says nothing of reception he met with when he returned home to Sugar City. It does not say if he received a plaque, or a medal. A trophy? A certificate? When I asked him if there was an award, he shrugged; he couldn't remember. Whatever it was, it vanished.

Willie's cornet, too, vanished. The next year Will Johnson moved his wife, five children and his nephew, Roy, to the northwest corner, the panhandle of Idaho, Coeur d'Alene to join Roy's father, George Johnson. "Can you imagine," Bill wrote in "My Life," "six kids and two adults with all their worldly belongings in an old Chrysler? First car we had with glass windows. My Dad painted a house for the car. It wouldn't run, but he fixed the motor and we started out to make the trek." There were so many people in the car that Bill, the eldest, spent the whole trip on the running board. I have a tiny, wizened snapshot taken on this journey. It's suppertime and the five children are sitting cross-legged in front of some brush, eating bread and possibly jam. Mae kneels in front of them with a tin and an open jar in the grass beside her. Her back is to the camera and beyond her you can see the long, sharp shadow of the car and at the edge of that shadow, in bold relief against the brush, there is a huge iron frame bed. Not a mattress, just the frame. My dad says they brought the bed because "Ma wouldn't sleep on the ground." Presumably the rest of them slept on the ground. That last night on the road they "stayed near a restaurant built to resemble a fish," before going on to Squaw Bay to live in a log cabin.

In 1991, my kids, my parents, Uncle Frank and I found this restaurant that resembled a fish. The siding on it was made to look like scales, the open mouth the door. Frank lived in nearby Spokane, and he had done some scouting, and found the log cabin on Squaw Bay. We drove up the hill to the cabin and the people who lived there (!!!!) very kindly let us look around. Much had changed, but the cabin, improved, electrified and now with running water, still stood.

In 1936 when Will and his tribe arrived in their Chrysler with the bedframe strapped to the top, George Johnson and another son were already living in the cabin. Neither Frank nor my dad could remember why George was there, or who the cabin actually belonged to. (George had married a New Jersey girl he met while serving in the Great War; she returned to Idaho with him, but, no surprise, not for long. She left him with two kids, another of those unspoken divorces.) For the ten people in that small space, housekeeping would have fallen on Mae. Water had to be fetched uphill from the lake in buckets. That was Bill's job. As he brought buckets up from the lake, he remembered stepping around piles of bear shit in the woods, though he never saw the bear. They stayed in the Squaw Bay cabin for the summer, and of that summer, the lake, the woods, the long sunny days, the gaggle of high spirited kids, one can imagine the adventures. (One of Bill's sisters once told me that some twenty-five years later she and her husband were having a drink in a bar on Coeur d'Alene lake, and some old duffer came up to her and said, "You're one of the Johnson girls, aren't you?" He remembered her from that summer.)

In the fall Bill's family left Squaw Bay and moved to town. The half-of-a-house they rented—ominously located at the corner of Lost and Dollar—had electricity. Bill, a high school student, got a job every Saturday morning cleaning out pipes in the high school furnace for twenty-five cents an hour. With this money he made the payments on a new trumpet. Did he sell Willie's cornet? Did the crack finally break the bell open? When I asked him, sadly, he had no memory of its fate. I, personally, like to think there is some special heaven for musical instruments that have changed people's lives, some place where they are all redeemed from celestial pawn shops, and that this cornet, cracked bell and all, is played by some joyous and deserving soul.

VIII

At Coeur d'Alene High School in addition to music Bill took typing, chemistry, Spanish, history, and English. His passion for the trumpet continued. "I wasn't much of a student in high school," he admits in "My Life." "I practiced the trumpet from one to four hours at a time. I used to carry my mouthpiece around and play only with the mouthpiece for my lip muscles. In this way it was not difficult to hit and hold a high-C which was my intention when I used only the mouthpiece to blow." His grades were lousy, a fact he would later rue. All through high school he had numerous jobs besides Sundays in the high school furnace room. He cut lawns; he carried hod for a builder, hoisting cement in a wooden trough; he worked for a hardware store in town. Weekends he played trumpet in a roadhouse on the shores of Coeur d'Alene lake. (We found the roofless, overgrown ruin of this place on our 1991 jaunt too.) My dad said he stood on an overturned crate there, and blasted that trumpet, probably not Herbert L. Clarke anymore, more likely jazzy tunes ala Louis Armstrong. He always admired Louis Armstrong, though how or where he would have heard his music, I don't know. Bill himself bought the first radio the Johnsons ever had.

The Depression was a disaster for many, but for the young and fit and restless, particularly young men, New Deal programs offered opportunities. After high school Bill worked for the Civilian Conservation Corps (CCC) in the forests fighting blister rust on trees. He hitchhiked back to Coeur d'Alene with his first paycheck, and bought the radio mentioned above, along with a couch and an overstuffed chair that were delivered to his mother, the first new furniture Mae Johnson had ever had. Bill also rode the rails and hitchhiked around the West with a friend. At the end of that summer, he bought a Model T for fifteen dollars and said goodbye to Coeur d'Alene forever. He returned to southern Idaho, to Rexburg to go to Ricks College.

Ricks College began in the 1880's as an academy so that Mormon children wouldn't have to go to school with the Gentile locals, but by the 1930s it was at least a two year college (it is now Brigham Young University-Idaho). Though his high school grades were below average, Bill talked his way into Ricks. He lived in the car till the weather got cold and then he lived in the basement of a laundry. "All I had," he writes, "was determination and a goal and the willingness to work long hours to accomplish my dreams of the future."

Attending Ricks College might have been the fulfillment of a childhood dream, but the place seems to have inspired him mainly to hi-jinks. He and three other rowdy college boys got into mischief. They turned over the night watchman's outhouse—with the night watchman in it. They lured a cow into the library late one night and in the morning they watched from afar, laughing their asses off, as administrators, librarians, and janitors tried to make the cow go down the stairs. The culprits were discovered (I don't know how) and these antics would have gotten them all expelled, but one of the partners in crime was the son of a prominent Mormon family, and so all three were spared.

Shortly thereafter, Bill's uncle, Archie Henderson (the one who had looked so confident in the 1908 photograph) approached him with the opportunity to go to Utah State. Archie lived in Utah and Bill could use his address for in-state tuition. Bill leapt at the opportunity. For him, this choice, the chance to go the University at Logan, was the end of larks in the library, turning over outhouses, of aimless hitchhiking and riding the rails. This was the beginning of adulthood where the values and tactics and determination he had first practiced with Willie's cornet would coalesce to shape his future.

Before he could enroll at Utah State University in the fall of 1941, Bill was in an automobile accident, a bad one. I do not know the particulars. Following the accident, he suffered a ruptured appendix and was operated on by a drunken doctor at a Utah hospital who didn't know how to use anesthesia. Not only could Bill not attend Utah State, his recovery from the operation was long and painful. He recuperated for months at Archie Henderson's house where Archie and his wife generously looked after him.

Bill was lying on the couch in his uncle's livingroom listening to the radio in December 1941 when news came on that the Japanese had bombed Pearl Harbor. Archie Henderson stood up, clutched his heart and fell to the floor. The Hendersons had twin sons in the navy. Both on the USS Arizona. Archie's wife, hearing Archie cry out, rushed in and saw Bill bending over her stricken husband, heard the president talking of the attack at Pearl Harbor and froze in the doorway, urine running down her legs and pooling on the floor. One of the Henderson sons lived. One son died on the *Arizona*. Archie died in Bill's arms.

After Archie's funeral Bill hitchhiked to Utah State University at Logan. The accident and hospital bills for the ruptured appendix took all the money he had saved for tuition. For the spring term, 1942, Bill talked the Dean into taking a promissory note for tuition and books. He got a job in Ogden where he worked nights, twelve hours; he put a used typewriter for down payment on a car that would let him drive to the job. He was to have joined a fraternity, but couldn't now. Still he talked the fraternity house into letting him crash there. So unique was Bill Johnson that in spring 1942 the college newspaper published an unsigned feature article with these and his other exploits.

It's the Best Man who Wins; Youth Proves Adage Truthful

This is a story of a youth. The author is not Horatio Alger and the hero is not the legendary Frank Merriwell, but a student of this school. Here is the story.

His thumb waved in the cold wind which wildly whipped his coat around him. The passing motorist stopped and he hopped in. He was on his way to college.

Three days later the traveler reached Logan. "I'm glad I made it," he mused as he jingled the 33 cents in his pocket. The money he jingled was all he had. Successively an auto accident and an appendectomy at the Budge hospital the preceding fall quarter had taken all he had saved for school.

It was as cold as January days are in Logan and his first thought was for shelter. "I'd better find a place to live," he thought, and shouldering his suitcase made his way to the fraternity house where he had pledged before financial difficulties forced him to drop. "Fellows," he explained, "I'm broke and would like to stay here. I'll pay you when I can."

"Okay. But you're crazy," was the answer when they learned of his plans.

"Maybe," he replied.

The next day he hitched to Ogden and talked himself into an afternoon job at the depot. He had a job, but needed a car to get to it. After much discussion, he convinced a local auto dealer that a new typewriter was as good as a down payment, and drove away in an old '30 model Chevrolet. The tires were thin, the motor tired, and the wiring worked only on occasion, but it would run. It would carry him to work.

When he registered for school he talked the officials into taking a note for tuition and books, and renewed his climb up the ladder up of education.

For two quarters this lad spent twelve hrs. six days a week at work. During this time, he carried a full school load (often staying up all night after work to do an assignment) and received better than average grades. He also paid for his car, paid off his notes, his living expenses and three hundred dollars on his hospital bill. He worked up from laborer to clerk at the depot and

had an offer of special training from them to enable him
to receive an important position there. These things he
did, and the amazing thing is, that he did it after being
near death from a ruptured appendix and lying in bed
for three months.

Today he is back to school, wearing that wide smile on
his face. A senior from Coeur d'Alene, Idaho, he is in
the Marine Reserve, and a social climber, and is very
active in politics or athletics. He is just another guy—His
name? Oh, yes, I nearly forgot. His name is Bill Johnson.

Ricks had not inspired him, but at Utah State Bill Johnson first formed the dream of becoming a doctor. He discovered that he loved science, especially medical science,
an enthusiasm that never left him. He loved studying too,
and threw himself into coursework (while, at the same
time, looking after his teenage brother, Frank). Bill graduated with a BA in physiology.

After World War II, pursuing his dream of becoming
a doctor, he applied to medical school; he was rejected
because of his high school grades. That's what he told me.
Knowing him as I did (as an adult) knowing his determination and perseverance, 1 was surprised he had not fought
this rejection. I asked why did he not apply elsewhere if the
first place turned him down. Try some other school? He
had no answers for my questions. Perhaps circumstances
intervened; after all, when the war ended he was a married
man with a small child. He used the GI Bill to get a Masters
in Public Health at Cal Berkeley. Harry Truman spoke at
his 1947 graduation.

Bill Johnson worked for thirty years as pharmaceutical rep, but he would never be a doctor. If playing "Bride of the Waves" to win the Idaho State competition was a bright dream realized, rejection from medical school was, remained, a dream bitterly unfulfilled, a failure that rankled for the rest of his life.

World War II also shaped the man he became. Without the social upheavals that conflict inflicted upon his whole generation, Bill Johnson would probably never have left the Mormon enclaves of his youth. Right after graduation from Utah State, the Marines sent him to train at Parris Island, South Carolina, an experience of which he never spoke, and yet was crucial to his life. Here he met Sid Finegold, a Jewish guy from LA who had also joined the Marine Reserve in college and was called up right after he graduated from UCLA. Had my father ever before met anyone Jewish? I doubt it. But they struck a lifelong bond. Sid became his best friend, so close that I was probably seven or eight before I knew we weren't actually related to Uncle Sid. Sid was best man at my parents' wedding, and in 1994 he came to Washington to celebrate their fiftieth wedding anniversary. Sid told me that at Parris Island the two of them were in training to be officers to be sent to the European Theatre of Operations. Sid and Bill did not want to go to the ETO where life expectancy for officers was not great. They took a demotion (they would never be officers) and transferred to the Navy. Bill became a pharmacist's mate on an aircraft carrier, the USS Bairoko, plying the Pacific. The two were stationed at Long Beach, and made frequent jaunts into Los Angeles where Sid's family lived. Sid was with Bill at a USO dance in March 1944 when he met petite USC student, Miss Peggy Kalpakian. He told Sid, "I'm going to marry that girl."

By then Bill Johnson had put the Mormon church entirely and firmly behind him. He smoked cigarettes, he drank coffee and tea and alcohol, his best friend was Jewish. He told Peggy Kalpakian's father that though he had been raised Mormon, he had no religion. Was this denial the result of careful mulling, deciding or declining the religion of his youth based on its merits or his own convictions? I doubt it. He was not an introspective man. I suspect that after 1941 as he moved into the great world, he simply sloughed off the church and its teachings, putting all that, along with his poverty-stricken past, behind him, never alluding to it. He had also put the trumpet and music behind him. Why, I do not know. When I asked, he simply shrugged.

Peggy Kalpakian Johnson did not learn of his youthful dedication, his enthusiasm for the trumpet till they had been married for about ten years. One afternoon Bill came home from work besotted with brass, thrilled to show off a trumpet he had bought for $100! My mother was appalled! Bill's salary was $325 a month, and $100 was twice their mortgage payment. (Double your own rent or mortgage payment, and think on that for some little glimpse of what she felt. Moreover she was constantly juggling the needs of three little children on limited funds, and they needed a new water heater.) She was furious at this squanderous extravagance, money he had outright blown, wasted cavalierly, and without even consulting her. And for what? A brass instrument? More humiliating yet, the check bounced. The people called to complain, and my mother offered to return the trumpet, but they declined. They wanted the hundred dollars. My mother went to the bank, and covered the check from their savings. The water heater would have to wait.

Other than the novelty of his bringing it home in the first place, I have no recollection of my dad playing this trumpet. Perhaps his technique was rusty. More likely my mother's anger was ongoing and unsoftened. My mother thinks he eventually sold it and didn't tell her, just as he had bought it and didn't tell her. That poor trumpet is not in the special heaven for instruments that have changed people's lives.

IX

I can't help but wonder if that lack of support from his own family helped to fuel my dad's tireless enthusiasm for my sons' musical education. He and my mom drove Bear and Brendan to piano and sax and trumpet lessons (and out for ice cream afterwards). They drove the kids to musical competitions in other towns when I was working. My dad and his video camera were a familiar sight at every recital, every performance of the high school jazz band, every hometown parade they were in with the marching band.

In the midst of these busy years, and after hearing my dad's cornet stories, I gave him a trumpet for Christmas 1989. A school band instrument, nothing special, but the sight of it, gleaming in its case, swaddled in blue velvet lining, clearly pleased him. He was delighted, and put it to his lips, though at seventy years old he could only squawk out a few notes. When Bear started band in middle school, my dad gave him the trumpet. Bear played it all through middle school and high school, and into college. It did not change his life, but it got him his first bit part on screen when make-up people pasted fake sideburns on his cheeks and he appeared as a trumpet player in 1970s band playing backup in the TV movie, *The Sonny and Cher Story.*

For my dad's eightieth birthday in 1998 I ordered a CD of vintage recordings, Herbert L. Clarke himself playing "Bride of the Waves" and other cornet classics. My parents came to my house, and I said, "Sit down. I have a surprise for you!" I set the CD play to Track 4, "Bride of the Waves." As the first few bars wafted out of the speakers, he looked stunned, truly stunned, as though he had been punched in the gut, and was dazed and disoriented. Then his eyes lit with something close to jubilation. And then he put his face in his hands and began to sob.

I had never seen him cry.

Bill Johnson was dying for a long time. Heart bypass surgery in 2003 from which he never truly physically re-covered. The stroke in 2005 at first did not seem major; his mobility was only slightly affected, his mind more so, but within months, clearly, the damage had accelerated, and would get worse yet. He fought dementia in the only way he knew how, working tirelessly toward an imagined goal, making lists, long detailed notes, systems of the body, as though he were studying for an exam in a phantom anatomy class, somehow reliving the medical school he had never attended. He wrote "books" about the signs and effects of diabetes and stroke, complete with diagrams and charts. He insisted that my mother make copies, staple them, and give them out to everyone in the family. We all had to thank him profusely. He wrote "poems" (lacking meter, but not heart) long odes about "The Quest for Knowledge," and other inscrutable undertakings. The most famous poem, "Why," includes the line, "Why do I have 17 billion miles of DNA? I could probably get by fine with three...." These lines cracked us up. Bear and Brendan set these immortal lyrics to music, and performed for him. (And for a while they had a quintet called 17 Billion Miles of DNA that performed in small LA jazz clubs.) My dad scrawled on the backs of envelopes ordering us to mail these missives to all sorts of people, to do it now, immediately, today. (We didn't and said we did.) He fell in love with certain words and would write them and their definitions on anything that came to hand, including walls and lampshades and sheets. For a man who had always been generally upbeat, even funny, he grew increasingly difficult and demanding, sour and angry.

He had outlived his whole generation, all his siblings, all their spouses, and many of his forty-odd first cousins. When his brother Frank died in April, 2011 we did not tell him because if he could fathom the loss, it would devastate him, and if he could not fathom it, well, what was the point?

For six years my mother looked after him at home: his meds, his meals, his need for pens and Wite-Out. By summer, 2011 he was so feeble he could not or would not eat. We called in hospice, and moved him to a care center. Here Bill's many needs were met by a caring and competent staff, and to everyone's surprise, he lived another fourteen months. They called him The Comeback Kid. Though his body came back from the brink of death, his mind did not recover. Still, his mood improved and though he could be sullen, he wasn't generally sour or angry, and he always recognized us when we came to visit.

I brought in a little CD player and often played "Bride of the Waves" and "Carnival of Venice" and other trumpet and cornet classics for him. He would beam, and tell us over and over the oft-repeated stories: his constant practice on the cornet and the trumpet, his never having had a lesson, winning in Pocatello, becoming the best trumpet player in the whole state of Idaho. Just days before he died we put "Bride of the Waves" on the CD player. He closed his eyes as the music wafted out. He smiled, paused, waited, his finger pointing skyward for that last, sweet high-C note that he had so faithfully practiced nearly eight decades before, a note that Herbert L. Clarke holds flawlessly in one trembling breath. And when "Bride of the Waves" ended, he smiled, and said that Anetta had given him a cornet, that it had once belonged to her husband, Willie. He said they were waiting for him.

CHAPTER THREE

THE UNBELIEVERS

"No rest for the wicked and the righteous don't need it."
~Mormon Proverb

I

Los Angeles, a September evening, 1944. The windows are open, and the sounds of traffic from Olympic Boulevard float up and flutter the long voile curtains in the living room. Two demitasse coffee cups sit on a tray. Bill Johnson has come to ask Harry Kalpakian for his daughter's hand in marriage. Bill wears his navy uniform. Harry is in his eternal starched white, long sleeved shirt, and a vest. My father and grandfather are about to have this formal discussion in a state of mutual happy ignorance.

In this conversation the cataclysmic events that had brought Harry Kalpakian to Los Angeles would not have been alluded to. Bill Johnson, for his part, knew squat about the Armenians, of their two thousand year history, nothing of the Armenian Apostolic Church, maybe not even that there was such a thing, since my mother and her sisters all went to the Methodist church. He knew nothing of the Ottoman Empire and their persistent persecutions of the Christian minority within their borders. He knew the phrase, the Starving Armenians. Everyone knew that. Harry Kalpakian would not have begrudged Bill Johnson his ignorance on the subject. Indeed, he might have welcomed it.

And what did Harry know of the Mormons? Harry had only been in America since 1923, only been a US citizen since 1931. He knew nothing of the Mormons' peculiarly American history, knew nothing of their belief that God had given Joseph Smith a new gospel and that Jesus had walked the North American continent, or that their practices included baptism for the dead, and had once included plural marriage. He knew nothing of the Saints' strictures against coffee, tea, alcohol, tobacco and Coca Cola. (Bill smoked Pall Malls and drank all of those substances.) Harry Kalpakian probably thought the Mormons were Protestants. Like the Methodists.

My father also welcomed Harry's ignorance. Besides, Bill had forsaken the Saints, put them and his hardscrabble, impoverished past behind him, not, in my opinion as an act of overt intellectual rebellion, more likely as a result of riding the tide of history. Were it not for World War II Bill might never have seen the ocean, or had a Jewish best friend or be asking a Los Angeles grocer if he could marry a girl who was born in Constantinople, Turkey, a girl who was herself a naturalized citizen.

As the story of that conversation has come down to me, Harry Kalpakian asked Bill Johnson: what religion would any children be brought up in? Bill replied something to the effect that he didn't care about religion. He had been raised a Mormon, but he had no religion whatever; Peggy could raise any children they had as little heathens if she wished. This latter was probably not the answer my grandfather wanted, and Bill would have seen as much in his face, would have corrected himself quickly, and replied respectfully, and truthfully, that he had no objections to the Methodists.

This would have been enough for my grandfather. After all, Harry and Helen Kalpakian had a religiously mixed marriage. He was Apostolic, she was Congregationalist. They had married against the objections of both his family and Miss Towner. Harry and Helen were pragmatic rather than dogmatic; their daughters were not raised Congregationalist nor Apostolic. They were Methodists because from their house on Haas Avenue, they could walk to the Methodist church.

So my grandfather gave his consent, and two weeks later, in September 1944 William Jess Johnson and Peggy Kalpakian were married by the naval chaplain in Long Beach. A wartime wedding in which the groom wore his naval uniform, and the bride wore a smart lavender suit with the broad shoulders of the era, a broad-brimmed hat and a gardenia tucked in her hair. Sid Finegold, Bill's best friend was the best man, Betty Kalpakian, the maid of honor. Angagh

Kalpakian was there as well, and some guy whose name no one can remember. They drove back to the Kalpakian home on Olympic Boulevard for a reception. (Which, oddly, they did not even mention to the youngest Kalpakian daughter, Harriett, age nine; she noted rice on the steps when she came home from her friend's house. Why was that?) The newlyweds had a brief honeymoon in Santa Barbara and came back to a little apartment.

The War, as my mother is fond of noting, changed everything. Without having lived through it, who can re-imagine the intensity of the experience, or why, a college student might marry a man she had only known for six months. Four months after that wedding, in January, 1945 the *USS Bairoko* shipped out to the Pacific, and Bill was gone. Peggy, now pregnant, gave up the apartment, dropped out of USC because pregnant women, even married ones, did not attend university. She moved back into her parents' house, took piano lessons, and learned to play "Clair de Lune" which may account for my fondness for Debussy.

Nine months after the wedding, I came into the world. When Peggy's labor pains came, my grandmother drove her all the way to the Naval Hospital in Long Beach where as the wife of a navy man, treatment was free. She went through thirty-six hours of labor without any kind of painkiller or preparation, and scarcely even any doctor's attention. They said they needed the doctors and the nurses and painkill-ers elsewhere. Anyone could have a baby. She brought me home to my grandparents' house to the doting delight of the whole family and we lived there awaiting the end of the War in the Pacific.

The *USS Bairoko* returned to Long Beach in October 1945, blew its triumphant whistle and began off-loading the sailors. I imagine Peggy standing with the other women of her generation. I hope she had a gardenia for her hair. I hope she had a new suit, and smart shoes and one of those wartime hats that she would have held on to when the stiff breeze came up off the sea. The War was over, and a new life together would begin. Did she wonder about her husband, the father of her child, with whom she had only shared four months of married life? I hope that the sight of the handsome sailor, Bill Johnson, coming off the *USS Bairoko* diluted the taste of her dashed hopes for college graduation. I hope she flew into his arms, and that they held each other close, wept, laughed, kissed, and that the joy of this reunion sustained her for years to come.

II

Postwar peacetime in a land of plenty: fifty dollars down, fifty dollars a month, for thirty years, two possible models, three possible colors. Vets move in free. Done! In 1951 and for $10,000, my parents bought a house on Beckford Avenue, a brand new tract in Reseda, in the San Fernando Valley. It came with a fridge, a stove, a washer, a clothesline outside and an incinerator behind the garage. The houses in this tract, long straight blocks lined up perfectly, were plunked down amid what had once been alfalfa fields, chicken ranches and pear orchards. Any such ranches, fields or orchards that still stood nearby would be soon

razed for more houses just like them. On Beckford Avenue
the neighbors were all white people, an odd assortment,
people who had flocked to California either because of the
war, or simply to re-invent themselves.

Beckford Avenue was the very picture of White Bread
Eden, of Dad-and-Mom-and-Kid-Land, the smiling ads,
bland, benign images of the Fifties. Dad left in the morning to go to work. Mom stayed home with the kids, me, my
brother, Doug, born in 1950, my sister, Helen, born in 1952,
another brother, Brian, born in 1957. These neighborhoods
had at least three kids to a home. Some of the boys were
little thugs-in-training, but most of us were great friends.
We all had cowboy hats and holster sets with cap pistols to
swagger about and shoot one another, to take turns falling
down dead and getting up again without a second thought.
Girls and boys had Davy Crockett coonskin caps, and everyone could sing the "Davy Crockett" theme song, and
just about everyone on Beckford had a television set. On
hot afternoons we could sit near the swamp cooler and
watch cartoons on local channels, and kids' programming
like *Sheriff John's Lunch Brigade, Engineer Bill*, crude pup-
pet shows like *Beanie and Cecil* (the Seasick Sea Serpent)
or *Thunderbolt the Wonder Colt, The Mickey Mouse Club*,
and TV serials like *Robin Hood* and *The Cisco Kid*. Sad to
say, while I have forgotten much that was important, and
all the math I was ever taught, these theme songs remain
fried into my brain.

On the tide of postwar prosperity, Bill Johnson had found
a good job as a pharmaceutical rep for Lederle Laboratories,

a division of American Cyanamid. Lederle gave Bill $325 a month to start with, as well as a company car—a Ford or a Chevy—every other year. He racked up a lot of miles, driving all over greater LA selling medicines and vitamins to doctors and pharmacies and hospitals. He was charming, professionally knowledgeable about his products, and he did very well. He had ambitions too, but when Lederle offered him a promotion to district manager in Hawaii, he turned it down, and after he declined, Lederle never offered him another opportunity. His wartime experience in the South Pacific (of which, I should add, he never spoke) left him with no wish whatever to return. Even many years later when I lived in Hawaii, my mother, my sister and my youngest brother came to visit, but my dad did not want to come.

In the 1950s there were so many kids taxing the Los Angeles school system, they skipped some of us ahead. As a result, I missed the second half of kindergarten (probably why I never quite learned to stand in line properly). Shirley Avenue School, new bungalows hastily plunked down, instantly filled with white kids from all these housing tracts. The teachers (with one notable, charming, eccentric exception) were all young with freshly-minted degrees, courtesy of the GI Bill. In addition to the elderly eccentric, my other favorite teacher was Mr. McDonald, young, cheerful, full of energy and warmth. Best of all, he gave lots of our fourth grade class time to art, and he himself was a wonderful illustrator. I remember asking him if he would illustrate my books for me when I wrote them. He very kindly agreed. (At this same time I asked my mom if she would type them for me, and she agreed, and it should be duly noted that she did. For some twenty-five years she used her wonderful typing skills on my manuscripts, and later, entered my rough drafts into the computer.) After the sixth grade I moved to Sutter Junior High, and here too, the schools were so overcrowded, we had split-session days. I went in the mornings. I remember waking in the dark, hearing the DJ on KMPC opening, as he always did, with Count Basie's "The Kid from Red Bank," and someone on the radio calling out, "Get off there you bums, or you don't get no hay!" (More composting trivia taking up brain space that could be better allotted.)

Except for upheavals—like the trumpet that cost two mortgage payments, and my dad's automobile accident in 1956—these sunny, undifferentiated years passed happily, unremarkably. We got a second car, a 1948 purple Chrysler. We spilled bird seed in it. We got a dog, a big slobbery boxer that my mother forbade in the house. My dad built a cement patio with a roof for protection from the sun, a patio big enough to roller skate on. He built an office for himself in the garage; he built a doghouse for the dog. He built a playhouse for me. He built bookshelves in the livingroom, and china cabinets high in the kitchen for my mom's lovely Lenox china. He put in a swing set. They planted fruit trees—peach, plum and apricot—that lavished us with fruit every summer, and a grape arbor so my mother had her own grape leaves for *derev*. My mom sewed all my clothes. She took me to see Mary Martin in *Peter Pan*. We went to Disneyland the year it opened, and rode the merry-go-round and the steamboat. Summers, my mother took us to the Piggly Wiggly market just for the air conditioning, and across the street to Rosie's Five and Dime (no air conditioning) where for a nickel you could buy sheets of paper with ghastly little pink candies you'd all pass round and peel off with your teeth. She took us every two weeks to the storefront public library on Sherman Way (also no air conditioning). We went to the Methodist church and I was baptized Methodist, an event I remember not for the solemnity of the rite (a few demure drops on the forehead) but for the family party afterward, the homemade *lamajune* and *derev*, the illustrated New Testament that my grandparents gave me, and the pretty dress my mother made.

In the midst of all that was ordinary, in January 1956 came word that my Mormon grandfather, Will Johnson, sixty-eight years old, had suffered a stroke in Ogden, Utah, and lay at death's door. I would feel the effects of this death, the death of the patriarch for the rest of my childhood, and beyond. The effects of Will Johnson's death would ripple into my creative life for decades.

III

When Bill Johnson returned home two weeks after his father died, he had undergone—in the Shakespearean phrase—a sea change. Pale, shaken, he looked at us, his wife and children, as though he had returned not from Ogden, Utah, but from the unruly past, that foreign country. My mom and I watched, eyes wide, perplexed, as he poured his coffee into a saucer, blew on it to cool it, and drank it from the saucer. He didn't even sound like himself. He had absorbed his relatives' countrified diction on the order of "We was. . .", "It don't. . ." "Ain't..." and the like. He spoke in his own voice, but these were not his words. Who was this strange person?

When he was in Utah for those two weeks he telephoned my mother, but they could talk only briefly because long distance was expensive. Peggy had little idea of what he was actually going through. He did, however, tell her that he had arrived at the Ogden hospital in time to hold his father's hand, but Will never regained consciousness, never spoke again.

For the funeral, January 14, 1956 mourners assembled at Lindquist and Sons mortuary in Ogden. All of Will's five children and their spouses (except for my mom) and some of their grandchildren were present. I can imagine the front pew, Mae Johnson with damp eyes and trembling lips, flanked by her daughters, Evelyn, Leila, and Elaine and their husbands. The room filled as well with many of Will's nine siblings, and their spouses, and children. Many had traveled long distances to be here. (Will was the first of his generation to die; his brothers, George, Leslie and Stan would all die within eighteen months.) Beyond this large phalanx of family, the room filled with respectful, admiring Saints. So distinguished was Will Johnson that he was mourned by people from the many Wards where he had served as Elder, choir director, youth group director, and in many other capacities for the church, to say nothing of his genealogical work, and temple rites. Two Ward bishops spoke at his funeral as well as the Stake president. (The Ward was the Mormon equivalent of a parish; several wards comprised a Stake.) Indeed, so devout and renowned a Saint was Will that someone typed up the entire funeral service including everyone's remarks and the lyrics to the hymns, bound and stapled this eighteen-page document. Thus, I actually have it in hand; I know what was said, and sung.

The eulogy—a long, loving personal tribute—was given by Howard Hale, Will's uncle by marriage. Hale had married Jeannettie Johnson's sister in 1893. In 1906 Howard Hale had joined the brand new Ricks Academy in Rexburg, Idaho as a teacher. Howard prevailed on Will's parents to let him come with him and his wife to Rexburg, and attend Ricks. Howard says Will finished his high school there (in 1906 he would have been nineteen) and went on to two years of college.

I have the formal portrait of Will Johnson, graduate of Ricks Academy given to me by Lila. It's a lovely studio photo of a seated young man dressed in a suit, holding in one hand a rolled up diploma, ribbon and all, and flanked by a vase of calla lilies. He looks dignified, pleased and proud. In 1998 I was putting together a big birthday book for my father's eightieth birthday, and I wrote to Ricks (now Brigham Young University-Idaho) asking for pictures and information. They generously sent me two pictures of Bill Johnson from the yearbooks. However, when I inquired after my grandfather, William Andrew Johnson, Jr., Ricks had no record of him as a student. Absolutely none. Nothing close to that name in that era. Howard Hale, yes; they said Howard Hale was on the faculty in those early years. So perhaps Howard Hale brought Will to Ricks, and he took the classes without ever formally enrolling (or paying). Perhaps Will's studio portrait was intended to suggest graduation rather than document it.

"I have known Will Johnson for sixty-two of his sixty-eight years," Brother Hale began. His eulogy says that Will started teaching, in a rural one-room school that had accommodation, a little apartment for the teacher at the back. He must have quit teaching by 1914, however because when he married Mae in December 1914, he brought her to a place he was homesteading near Woodrow, Idaho. Will taught again in Coeur d'Alene in the late 1930s where he conducted classes for, says Howard Hale, "aliens [who] were being taught the things that were necessary for them to know in order to get their naturalization papers." (The very sorts of classes my Armenian grandparents took in Los Angeles to qualify for citizenship.) Of those difficult, pinched years in and around Sugar City, those years of my father's childhood and youth, Brother Hale says nothing.

"If I was going to epitomize in just a few words William's life," he continues, "I would say—a great teacher, a marvelous musician both with voice and instrument, an artisan of the highest degree and a friend of everyone who came within the circle of his acquaintanceship . . . If someone wanted a plumbing job done or build a house or cabinet, he would do it. He built a house for me and we lived as neighbors to each other. He then became an expert draftsman and that was the work he was doing when he was called away." (i.e., died). Hale lauds at length Will Johnson's Saintly life, his dedication to the church, evoking a man who was devout, educated, respected, accomplished, a musician, an artist, a scholar, in short, the man of undimmed moral grandeur, echoing the "portrait" that, until very late in life, my father believed in, and conveyed to us. In conclusion Brother Hale asks, "Will you follow Will's example?"

Hale's eulogy was followed by a long, solemn address by Stake President Heber J. Heiner Jr. He too lauds Will's "leading in teaching and music," and all the myriad ways in which he had fulfilled the church's commandments. Coming at last to the end of his long oration, Heber J. Heiner Jr. concludes, "We should always remember that [our parents] living or dead. . .have given us the best they had, been devoted to us, and in return all they ask is that we be honorable, productive and righteous. If we fail our parents we are indeed ungrateful, untrue and unprofitable, and if we. . . be not faithful to our parents, we may fail in the most important phase in life."

I can imagine Bill there in the front pew. Their words must have wrung his heart, struck his emotional solar plexus with a brutal sense of his own unworthiness: he had given up, rejected all the values his father, a morally great man, represented. I suspect Bill was stunned, not simply with grief, but trying to absorb the loss, trying to deal with overwhelming feelings of failure, of being ungrateful, untrue, and unprofitable, emotions he could not articulate. This weird gumbo of guilt, loss, shock—and even more terrifying—the obligatory, introspective assessment of his past, this was utterly new and foreign to him. Bill Johnson was in way over his head.

Though Will Johnson left very little in the way of material goods, there ensued bitter family fights over what ought to go to whom. Bill badly wanted the violin, and my grandfather's painstaking genealogical charts. However, his youngest sister, Elaine took them. Mae, in her wan way, said Bill should have them, but Elaine refused to give them up. Elaine was the most devout Mormon in the family, and I can see where the genealogy charts would have mattered to her, but the violin? Rancor from these 1956 feuds rattled for years. Elaine stayed on my dad's Shit List, off and on, until the 1980s. Elaine also took over the care and feeding of Mae who had so lived in Will's patriarchal shadow, she didn't know how to write a check. Within two years she had married again.

From Will's estate my father received the pocket metronome and his pocket watch. But he also received perhaps twenty long tubes that held drafts of Will Johnson's painstaking, elaborate Great Timetable reconciling in three long columns Biblical history, secular history and the history chronicled in the Book of Mormon. Three-eighths of an inch allotted to every twenty-five years since the beginning of recorded time. These were created with a draftsman's precision, blue paper, white ink. Draft after draft of these charts filled up these tubes, and it's impossible to tell which was the final, if indeed there was a final. Howard Hale says that Will began this undertaking while a student at Ricks, adding, "I don't know if he completed that work or not." Thus, according to Howard Hale, Will began in 1906, and he died in 1956. Fifty years. These charts represent a work of such historically scrupulous gravity that the brain aches to think of it. The reading required! Biblical history and events narrated in the Book of Mormon! To calibrate their exact chronological relationship to one another! The hours of drawing exacting lines! One error, one tiny slip, and he'd have to start all over. What would make him undertake such a demanding endeavor? Scholarly ambition? Religious zeal? I would never know the answers to these questions, but these Great Timetables would prove to be important, perhaps even central to my own creative life.

IV

Once he came home to California, as he navigated a deep abyss of grief and guilt, Bill Johnson accepted Howard Hale's challenge, and followed Will's example. He embraced the Mormon church, and he took us with him. Every Sunday. Mormon churches, at least in that era, had a generic sameness. Puritan-plain walls, blonde wood pews, narrow slits of windows tinted a greenish-yellow, and well-lit by overhead lighting fixtures. No room here for murky mysteries, or for the dimly beheld. None of those pale hymns the Methodists sang, like "Jesus Wants You for a Sunbeam." Oh no. The Mormons have their own hymnal, their own rousing songs, from the stirring "Welcome Welcome Sabbath Morning!" to the poetic promise of my particular favorite, "Now Let Us Rejoice." They had songs about the triumphs of Mormon pioneers, and the Celestial Kingdom and lips touching liquor and withering. In church cheerful Saints droned prayers, gave their two and half minute talks, swallowed bits of white bread and tepid tap water from tiny paper cups before they adjourned to separate Sunday School classes. The rosy-faced Saints called one another Brother and Sister. They all looked alike.

Though he dropped his relatives' countrified diction and quit pouring his coffee into a saucer to blow on it, still, for a man of high spirits, always ready to laugh, to make light of things, even serious things, my dad was newly somber My mother found this change in him alarming, appalling, even. She called her parents, asking for their counsel. They came over one day while Bill was at work, and she told them how strange was his behavior, but they were baffled, and not much help. I wonder if my grandfather thought back to his conversation with Bill that September evening in 1944 when Bill had shrugged at religion and suggested that he didn't care if his children were Methodists or heathens. In any event my grandfather, by way of comfort, said that Bill was acting out of grief and it would probably pass.

It did not.

The year after Will Johnson died, 1957, I was twelve, and Bill told Peggy I would need a white dress for my Mormon baptism. Did she remind him I had already been baptized Methodist? I don't know. But I remember the lovely white dress that she made for me for the ceremony which was held in a place where there were bleachers for the faithful, and it smelled of chlorine rather than sanctimony. I went under the engulfing waters, and emerged a member of the Church of Jesus Christ of Latter-day Saints. I vaguely recall standing up in church the following Sunday and getting a round of applause.

Thus, after Will Johnson's death the Sundays of my childhood split open like a melon. I went to the Mormon church in the morning and to the Kalpakians for lunch in the afternoon.

My grandparents' house was very unlike our little tract house. The rugs were old and colorful, the furniture was heavy and dark. There was in that house, despite the sunshine outside, an elusive undercurrent of sadness that was itself foreign. You could smell it in the closets where they kept the trunks they had brought from the old country, and in the foreign books lining the shelves in the small study. The Kalpakian kitchen, on the contrary, was a place of constant creation, of sensory delight which required no language, only energy, where my grandmother's hands fashioned a palpable past. These big family meals were as close to the old country as we would ever get because food alone escaped my grandparents' insistence on total assimilation. Food was the only thing they allowed into the present from the past.

Sundays afternoons we gathered at the dining room table which was massive, so high the littler children had to eat at a separate card table. My grandparents would sit at either end, all of us, aunts, uncles, cousins, lined up on either side. My grandfather said the Lord's Prayer in his heavily accented English. Each week, he would lift his wine glass to the assembled family and say, *Welcome to our house.*

After dessert (often handmade *paklava*) everyone moved into the livingroom, and my grandmother made coffee in the old country way and served it in demi-tasse cups. My grandfather passed around the lighter and the marble cigarette box. All the men lit up (except for him). The babies slept, mouths open, on their mothers' laps, the men lounged, shirtsleeves rolled up, my father's arm draped loosely near my mother's shoulder. Cigarette smoke rippled in thin blue banners against the cream-colored ceiling. Down the hall the younger children noisily raided the toy closet. Breezes from open windows picked up, carried the punctuating clink and ping of coffee cups. When they finished the coffee, they would turn the small cups over into the saucers, make a wish and turn the cup three times, then set it upright. My grandmother would, on request, tell your fortune from looking into the cup, and decoding a series of peaks and valleys into symbols of ....well, I do not remember what, nor do I remember anyone's fortune, only the laughter, the voices, accented and unaccented alike, the sound of traffic from Olympic Boulevard, the whole of it a comforting broth of sound and substance that seems to me, in retrospect, a gift.

V

Perhaps my father, having grown up in a patriarchal household, expected that his own home would function in that same way once he had decided to heed Brother Hale and follow Will's example. This did not happen. Peggy would never be like Mae, but having grown up with three sisters, and an adoring Daddy, Peggy didn't have the immediate tools to contest Bill. She gave up the Methodists without a fight, but she did not convert to the Mormons. She (and us, her children) accompanied him to Mormon services without complaint, at first in Reseda, and then attending the Second Ward church in San Bernardino. My dad was transferred there in 1958. (Transferred, not promoted.)

In San Bernardino my siblings were all baptized into the LDS church. My brother, Doug at age thirteen had the Aaronic priesthood conferred upon him. During my sister's serious illnesses the Elders came to her hospital room and performed "the laying on of hands," to heal her. Church activities filled up our summers. There was Primary for the little ones and Mutual Youth Group for me. I don't know what the boys did during Mutual Youth Group, but among the girls the good Sisters taught us to knit. All except me. They thought I was hopelessly all thumbs, and there was some truth in that, but more to the point, I refused to learn; knitting was something Mae Johnson did, and I had no intention of being anything like her.

Once a month the Ward Teachers came to our house. In my memory the Ward Teachers blend into a single face, one side old, one side young: pale, male, immutable faces that could never be differentiated one from the other. Brother Something and Elder Something. They all drove the same tan car. They spoke in the same droning voice. My mother always served lemonade.

As the eldest I'd often get roped into sitting through their visits. The Ward Teachers' primary function, as I saw it, was to make certain no one was having too good a time on this earth. Invariably they prayed, offered Saintly thoughts and quotes, and rattled on about the lesson for that month, perhaps something about the Word of Wisdom and how the human body was God's temple and how we Saints wouldn't want to defile that temple with smoking or drinking. I'd look around at the ashtrays all over the living room. My father had rejoined the church, but he had not given up coffee or cigarettes or the occasional cocktail or cold beer. By the time I was in high school my father would endure the Ward Teachers, but without enthusiasm, his elbows resting on his knees, fingers pressed together, eyes on the floor, and in need of a cigarette. He'd make the occasional, ineffectual joke. They would laugh in their pale way. But the Ward Teachers' main aim was to bring Sister Johnson, my mother, more wholly into the fold, to convince her to convert to her husband's faith, and go under the waters of baptism. Peggy practiced passive resistance tidied up to look like passive acceptance. *More lemonade, Elder?* Her good manners would not permit her to be other than polite. She perfected her tactic over years of practice: smile, listen, nod, *More lemonade, Elder?* Once a month. The Ward Teachers droned on, their bland voices solemn and sweet. She never ceased to decline and smile, smile and decline.

VI

I was obliged to listen to the Ward Teachers, to be as polite as my mother, but unlike her, I was not obliged to convert. I had been baptized after all. Gone under the waters, total immersion, at age twelve wearing the lovely white dress she had made for me. I was already entitled to the Celestial Kingdom, safely within the fold.

Every Sunday for several years we all went and sat in the main church for hymns and short talks and the scraps of dry white bread and the tiny paper cup of water, and then everyone went to Sunday School classes. The adults could choose what they wanted to learn. The children went by age. The class I attended was made up of thirteen and fourteen year olds, our hormones clanging like billiard balls, our unlovely bodies struggling out of childhood. Our teacher, Sister Bridges, invoked God's will and portrayed the penalties for social, physical, moral, spiritual and sexual transgression. She could not actually say the word *sexual*, so she touted sexual's other side, *purity*. One Sunday, as were leaving the classroom, and stirred by Sister Bridges' rhetoric—indeed, beatified by it—the girl walking beside me declared, "I'm never going to kiss a boy unless we're engaged."

"Well you know what," I retorted, albeit *sotto voce*, "the very first boy who kisses me, I'm going to kiss him back!"

Each week Sister Bridges conducted a sort of Sabbath-opera about the groveling of the unclean, the struggles of the righteous, and of course, the triumph of the Saints. She had a Wagnerian presence, a tall, broad-shouldered, massively-bosomed, handsome woman with two bold gray streaks in her dark hair that she kept severely pulled atop of her head, and knotted in a bun stuck with chopsticks that stuck out like antennae quivering on the lookout for sin. Sister Bridges could rattle off the begets and begats like they were her own relations; she could recite with the very knell of authenticity the dramas in the Book of Mormon, the battles of those wicked Lamanites, against the godly Nephites. She spake with an authority Moses would have envied (she was the mother of six) and with Moses's own knack for detail and hyperbole. So vivid and knowledgeable was Sister Bridges that when she talked about the afterlife, we could all be see the golden streets of the Celestial Kingdom filled with the many mansions Saints would inherit in heaven. In the Celestial Kingdom Saints could own property and have more than one wife. Celestial marriage included celestial procreation and thus, presumably, celestial intercourse (a peculiar fantasy for young teens). In the Celestial Kingdom families awaited the coming of Jesus, their collective conscience clean as their white garments while they lolled amid the milk and honey and many wives.

But Sister Bridges' hell, oh, her hell was unmatched! None of this sissy *purgatorio* for Latter-day Saints! Dante had nothing on Sister Bridges! Vivid, savage and structured is the Mormon hell! Time and all eternity is the Mormon hell! Time and all eternity is not just a phrase either, but concept central to the faith, closing every loophole, forbidding every exit. In Mormon hell the worst punishments are reserved, not for rapists and axe murderers, but for people who had been offered the Church of Jesus Christ of Latter-day Saints and who had actually declined! Lakes of fire and the devil's cackling delight in their suffering! No matter how Christian a life these people might lead, no matter how good or even saintly, by denying the doctrine of the Church of Jesus Christ of Latter-day Saints, the tortures of time and all eternity awaited them. After their deaths people who had spurned God's generous offer of the Restored Gospel—benighted Catholics, misguided Methodists, mindless followers of Orthodox mumbo-jumbo—would be wrenched from the arms of their Saintly loved ones. And no pleading on the part of the baptized could save them either. These church-denying dead would be cast down, down into a sea of flames, to drown in fire, to thrash and scream unceasingly, never to die or be released. Moreover, Sister Bridges implied, since we were all to be resurrected in the flesh, these hell-dwellers would continue to feel their pain, *in the flesh*. Her eyes would flutter and her enormous bosom heave with pleasure when she spoke of what would happen to Unbelievers in the Afterlife. She would all but chortle gleefully, and say, if you, or someone you knew had been offered the True Gospel and declined, or merely not accepted, oh, the grisly fate that awaited that person! We (the baptized Saints) would watch them burn and scream. Sister Briggs seemed to relish the prospect, as if it were theatre in which we would rejoice.

Inevitably, I grew woozy, nauseous like being in the backseat, and going up a twisty mountain road. None of the benign Ward Teachers had told my mother how, if she failed to convert to their religion, she would be plucked from us and cast down, and God not even caring what a wonderful person she was? *More lemonade, Elder?*

One Sunday I finally scraped together the courage to raise my hand and ask Sister Bridges about mitigating circumstances. Not my own personal mother, of course, though everyone knew I came from what was called a mixed marriage. But, for instance, Sister Bridges, what about the people who were already dead before God visited Joseph Smith? How could all those people be in hell when they didn't even know about the Latter-day Saints before 1825?

Sister Bridges replied majestically: *That is why we baptize for the dead, so as to give the dead the chance at heaven. That is the great gift of temple work! That is why the Saints are so dedicated to genealogy, why they go back, back, back through time and family records and collect all the family members, collect in fact all the people who ever lived before Joseph Smith. The Saints go under the waters of baptism for them and bring them into the Celestial Kingdom!* However, Sister Bridges also made it clear these dead could still be denied heaven if they stole, cheated, murdered, fornicated, broke oaths, forgot the Sabbath, bore false witness, worshiped false idols, committed adultery, coveted, lusted, blasphemed, or defied the Word of Wisdom given by God to Joseph Smith which forbade Saints to smoke, to drink spirits, wine, tea, coffee or Coca Cola. (I assumed God did not mention Coke by name in 1825, but some carbonated lake of transgression broad enough to include, say, Pepsi.)

One Sunday Sister Bridges brought God's Word of Wisdom home to us with a dark grandeur worthy of Ibsen. She drew from her purse a bottle of Coca-Cola and opened it. We were stunned. She also pulled out from her purse a nail, clean, gleaming, one of the biggest and certainly one of the nastiest nails in existence, and with her blunt fingers, she dropped it expertly into the bottle of Coke. She smiled at us knowingly and said: *Come back in a week.*

The following week we crowded around as she poured the Coke bottle over a bowl and, clank, out with the dreadful contents came the nail which she plucked from its brown bath and held aloft: rusted, hideous, mutated, a grotesque aberration of its former shining self. She plucked it from the bowl, passed it around. *If Coca Cola can do that to a nail, to solid metal, you kids just think what it will do to your flesh, your innards! You see this corrosion and corruption? You think about the corrosion of your body, the corruption of your soul!*

After these terrible episodes, these fiery possibilities, I always returned home dry-mouthed, white-knuckled, my skin prickling with anxiety. Corruption awaited my vital organs. My soul was putrefying with sin and Coca-Cola. My mother was going to hell for time and all eternity and we would all have to watch from heaven while she screamed. How Celestial could such a kingdom be? How could the Celestial Kingdom be pleasant when people you loved suffered, and you were powerless to protect them? Surely that has to be the worst experience ever, alive or dead. There was no one I could turn to for comfort, or even information. My mother and my grandparents didn't know what was in store for them. I certainly wasn't going to be the one to tell them.

I couldn't even ask my dad. After all, he smoked and drank and swore with an abandon that suggested he had forgotten just how disgusted God was with these lapses. God might smite Dad as well. But at least Dad was a baptized Latter-day Saint. Moreover he had done his patriarchal bit in bringing our little souls into the world and into the church. So even if Dad would not inherit many mansions in heaven, doubtless there was some northwest corner of the northwest corner, some tiny parcel of that celestial plain deeded to him for time and all eternity.

Week after week Sister Bridges soared to speak of the triumph of the Saints, how they would be given all that was promised to Joseph Smith. She waxed eloquent over the social, physical, moral and spiritual struggles besetting especially those who lived in darkness, like the Catholics and the Jews. (The Muslims were so benighted, they didn't even get mentioned.) She delighted in rhapsodizing about the afterlife where Dad and all his baptized kids would watch Mom writhe in hell. And in the course of listening to Sister Bridge's Cecil B. deMillean, Technicolor presentations I came to the conclusion that any heaven that wouldn't admit my mother, well, like Huck Finn, all right then, I'll go to hell! In my heart, in my mind, that was the end of it. I was fourteen.

VII

By the time I was in high school the truly terrible spasm of my father's grief at Will Johnson's death had eased. My mother had her Sundays returned to her. Dad would drive us to church, but most often he wouldn't go himself; he let us off, and went home, coming back to collect us when church was over. On these Sundays I would get out of the car, walk toward the church till I heard him pull away, and then I'd hotfoot over to the Thrifty Drug Store where I read magazines and used my collection plate money for Cokes. By the time I was sixteen, Mormon boys I knew had cars, and instead of attending Sunday School we'd drive up into the canyons, or over to the A&W for a root beer. Though I was always anxious, (in fact, dry-mouthed and white-knuckled) at the prospect of being caught getting out of the car instead of coming out of the church, my luck held. When my dad came to pick me and my siblings up, I was at the curb, and I could tell him without a single qualm that church was fine.

All this was part of a larger picture of adolescent rebellion. Growing up as a Mormon girl I resisted patriarchal domination long before the term patriarchy became something to be contested. My personal opposition to the patriarchy predated the Feminist Revolution, and it was reflexive, personal, not political. My father seemed to think that every possible teenage situation offered opportunities for unsanctioned wickedness. Under ordinary circumstances, I probably wouldn't even have taken these opportunities had I been presented with them, but since they were forbidden, they sparkled like the light gleaming on that very first Edenic apple. All through my adolescence my father and I were engaged in a struggle peculiar to willful personalities. I saw him as an unreasonable, over-strict tyrant, and he saw me as a disobedient brat, and we were both right.

That said, I never endured the ingrained bigoted assumptions about education that many girls lived with: that the boys in the family would have opportunities, and have them paid for, and the girls could just go to the junior college and shut up about it. My father had been thwarted in his dream to be a doctor, but he wanted his kids to be doctors. Going to university was a given when I graduated from high school at age sixteen. (I had been skipped twice in school, not for stellar performance, but because of overcrowded classrooms, courtesy of the Baby Boom.) But there was no point in even talking about a glamorous, expensive school like USC, not even UCLA, not anyplace where I would have to live away from home. There just wasn't any money for such extravagance. (Scholarships were not a possibility. My grades ran the gamut: A's in English, French, journalism and history, a good deal worse than that in science and math. A lot worse in math.) I went to University of California at Riverside, perhaps twenty miles away, paying the tuition with savings from my summer job at a title insurance company where I was a legal poster (basically, Bob Cratchit) for a whopping $200 a month.

UCR was the newest UC campus at the time, founded in the mid 1950s, architecturally uninspiring, even utilitarian, set about with skinny trees staked to posts. UCR had a reputation for attracting members of the Nerd Kingdom before there were Nerds, that is to say smart, socially awkward people. (I once met a guy from the Claremont Colleges who, without blinking a sexist eye, informed me that he had heard UCR girls had to take an Ugly Test to get in.)

The students were mostly middle-class white kids, some admittedly weird as owl pellets, most just as ordinary as I. A clean sweatshirt and clean jeans were considered the height of both fashion and hygiene.

I lived at home in San Bernardino, riding back and forth daily with a nerdy boy who also lived with his parents. At UCR I hung out in the library reading original *Harpers* magazines from the nineteenth century, a total outsider, no connections, no opportunities to make friends. At home I continued to be angry and difficult, feuding with my father until finally my grandmother intervened (presumably when my mother went to her bemoaning my bad attitude). My grandmother told my mother the situation was bad for everyone, and they had to let me go. Somehow the money was found and I lived in the dorms spring semester.

I can safely say I had more unfettered fun that seventeen-year-old spring than I have ever had in all my life, before or since. I made lifelong friends. The joy of having to answer to no one! Staying up all night! Staying out all night! Sneaking back into the dorms! (Oh yes, the women's dorm had a curfew; the men did not.) Groups of scruffy boys lived off campus, usually five or six of them in big, old rundown houses, the Lime Street Boys, the Blaine Street Boys, the Sixth Street Boys, and so on. (All these houses have long since fallen under the wrecking ball, replaced by respectable establishments, or parking lots.) At weekend parties the beer flowed, the music pounded and we all split out the back door when the cops came. If there was a choice between going to a lecture by the eminent philosopher

Paul Tillich, or drinking beer in the orange groves with a bunch of others—and there was—I chose the latter. I once told this story to someone who had known Tillich at the University of Chicago, and he said Paul Tillich would have chosen drinking beer in the orange groves too.

When my freshman year came to an end, I reluctantly moved home for the summer. That first Sunday morning in June, my father roused everyone. "Time to get ready for church!"

I hadn't planned this, but the proverbial now-or-never, was clear. I took a deep breath before I spoke. "I'm never going back to the Mormon church, and you can't make me."

A huge fight ensued, screaming, oaths, threats, the whole catastrophe. My father yelled that I ought to go, at the very least to set an example to my younger brothers and sister.

"If I'm the only reason they go to church," I retorted, "then maybe they shouldn't go either."

"Goddammit! I'll take them myself!"

"Do it!"

"You'll clean this whole house by the time I get home! Do you hear me?"

I did hear him, but I didn't clean the house, and when he came home the shit hit the fan again. My mother wisely stayed out of it; this was strictly between Dad and me.

I never again went to the Mormon church, and after this incident my adversarial relationship with my father eased as I moved into adulthood.

VIII

In truth, I never did have the makings of a Saint. A reflexive streak of high spirits and smart-ass rebellion in my nature contradicts their rigidly structured and wholly communal values, their smiling insistence on happy conformity. My mother and I, both unbelievers, handled the Mormons' demands, each in our own way. My mother with her unfailing politeness, *More lemonade, Elder?* Me, with the grandstanding declaration (which makes a good story, after all, and I am a novelist). Yes, I had disavowed the Mormons at fourteen, and dramatically cast them out my life forever at age seventeen, but to my great surprise, I have clung to them creatively. If on that Sunday morning some genie had whispered to me *Ha ha ha, Miss-I'll- never-go-to-church-again-and-you-can't-make- me! Ha ha ha, you twit. You'll never be free of the Mormons! They will stay with you, for decades!* I would have said: Impossible! And yet, the characters who first appear in *These Latter Days* and the town of St. Elmo have provided the backdrop for, or figured in half a dozen novels and I can't even count how many novellas and stories. Even minor figures (and their descendents) ripple from story to story like ghosts moving under the wallpaper.

In the fall of 1977 as I set about turning the story, *These Latter Days*, into a novel, my father let me take the many tubes of Will's Great Timetable to my Encinitas house. Once there I opened these tubes to find that each contained multiple, rolled-up drafts. The drafts billowed over the desk, on the floor, over the little guest bed in the room where I wrote. Like ocean waves cresting white, blue drafting paper, painstakingly inscribed in white ink, they surged in swells all around me. I was dazzled, shocked really. I felt a twinge of pity for this Casaubon-like undertaking that had clearly absorbed Will Johnson's very life, beginning in 1906 (according to Howard Hale) ending with his death in 1956. For fifty years, one slip of the pen, and he had to start anew. And he clearly kept his every draft. How did he know which one was current? Much less which one was final? Was there a final? None was so noted. When he died in 1956 he was working as a draftsman at Hill Air Force Base near Ogden. Did he labor all day over a drafting table and then come home and do the same at night? Was he poised there over his Great Timetable, pen in hand when he was seized by a stroke and rendered immobile? Was the prospect of death especially terrible knowing he would never finish this monumental undertaking? Though I felt no special affection for Will Johnson, he haunted me as for eight years (off and on) I researched, wrote, and revised *These Latter Days*, as I typed out endless false starts, unfinished endings, following tangents, developing and deleting characters in a book that I worked on for so long it had a nickname, TLD.

I always intended to dedicate TLD to my father. When at last my mom had typed the final draft (her glorious typing skills making beautiful manuscripts of my erratic drafts) she remarked to me, "It's a good thing you dedicated this book to your dad because when it comes out, he will need it. His family will give him hell."

Would the Johnsons feel betrayed? I wondered at this. Gulped a bit. After all, they had been kind to me, lavished me with stories and photographs and family lore when I visited them in 1977. Certain characters in TLD portray the strengths of the Mormons, especially Mormon women. But I knew that for the Mormon women of my actual acquaintance (especially Lila and Anetta) this was not the sort of Mormon story they would applaud. Some of the Saints in my novel are smug and money-grubbing, some are narrow, small-minded and spiteful. One, Samuel Douglass, the husband of the central character, Ruth Douglass, is mad, violent and cruel, crazed with power and prophecy, convinced that God gives him revelations. Ruth had married him because at twenty-five she was turning into that unthinkable anomaly, an unmarried Mormon woman. She's appalled to discover Samuel has lied when he takes her to live in a dugout in frontier Idaho. She bears six children, contending as well with hostile forces inside the church, and the hardscrabble community. In addition to his increasingly unhinged behavior and sexual demands, Samuel declares he will marry a plural wife and move all of them, including Ruth and her children to Mexico. Ruth makes a desperate escape taking her children with her. Leaving Idaho on the train, she eventually fetches up in St. Elmo, California, posing as a respectable widow. In St. Elmo she opens a restaurant and conducts a longtime love affair with the town's atheist doctor. She is tethered to the truth by lies.

However, Ruth was not the original central character. The book began as a thirty-page story, *These Latter Days*, centered on Miss Kitty Tindall, a 1911 Liverpool working class girl who converts to the Saints. Kitty emigrates to America, and marries a man named Gideon Douglass. Once Gideon's mother, the steely Ruth Douglass, strode into the narrative, she insisted this was her story. She fought me for years until I began to feel myself to be Ruth's servant rather than her creator. Ruth won this struggle because unlike Kitty, she had the strength to maintain a long, complicated novel. Kitty is demoted to a secondary character, and her Liverpool backstory diminished unto a paragraph. *These Latter Days* is not a cleanly streamlined book. Like much of my work it is baggy, observing chronology, but uneasy with regard to time, unruly, one might say. The story moves on and away from the proud, resolute Ruth, but the novel belongs to her.

My dad loved *These Latter Days*. He declared it the best book ever written. It's the only novel he ever read. (His favorite book was called *Vitamin E and Your Heart*.) By 1985 when *These Latter Days* was finally published, so far had Bill Johnson moved away from the burden of his father's death and his Mormon roots that the novel's critical portrayal of the church didn't matter to him. Nor did he mind that elements of his own family figured prominently in the story (the Great Timetable, the love story of Anetta and Willie, the dugout, the first brick house in a frontier county, a desperate wife fleeing an abusive husband on a train). What mattered is that I wrote it.

And the Johnson clan? On publication in 1985, we braced for their response. My mom told my dad that she would answer the phone for a while. To me, she said, "I'm ready for them." None of this *More lemonade, Elder?* crap. No more passive resistance tidied up to look like passive acceptance. She was ready to take on the Mormons to defend my novel!

But they never called. Not a word from Utah or Idaho. Not a word from Lila. (Anetta had died in 1982; Eva had died too.) Not a word from any of the other great-aunts or the one surviving great-uncle. Not a word from Mae, or any of my father's three sisters, or his brother, or his forty-odd first cousins. Did they read it? Did they even know it existed? I have to wonder. A bookseller friend who had worked in a Salt Lake City bookstore in 1985 told me *These Latter Days* was kept under the counter and would-be readers had to ask for it by name, and in a low voice, as if they too were heretics or unbelievers.

CHAPTER FOUR

WHY I DON'T WRITE FOR
THE NEW YORK TIMES

"Be True to Your School."
~The Beach Boys, 1963

I

W hen I look over the things I am proficient in and things I am not, I find that the best field for me to make a living in would be literary. I would like to become a free-lance writer." I wrote this in a ninth-grade essay titled, "My Future Occupation" for which I received an A+. Gratifying for the would-be writer. Moreover, I seemed, at age thirteen, to have had some understanding of the process working writers went through, agents, publishers, questions of rights and the like. I give my young self credit for the following insight:

There are really only five tools needed to become a writer. They are a typewriter, paper, a handy wastebasket, an imagination and patience. The typewriter is to write with, paper is

167

to write on, the handy wastebasket is not only for the often-received rejection slips, but also for the pages and pages of ideas that just won't work on paper.

This turned out to be, effectively, the story of my adult life.

At the very end of "My Future Occupation," I confessed that my real goal was to write a novel, a really good novel. However to be a novelist was such a vaunted ambition—like wanting to be a concert pianist or a movie star or a tight-rope walker—that I thought it best to aspire to become a freelance writer or a reporter, a journalist. And indeed, that's where I began, at San Bernardino High School, at the age of fifteen, on the staff of the *Tyro Weekly*.

The SBHS I attended, the buildings, came under the wrecking ball in about 1969. But when I went there, it still looked as it had when it was built in 1915, self-consciously academic architecture filtered through a Southern California aesthetic: long, covered, graceful arcades that connected three wings in the shape of "H." The broad staircases were steep; the walls were thick to protect from the blistering sun. By the time I attended, in the first wave of the Baby Boom, the school had long since outgrown its original "H" formation. The campus now had a separate cafeteria, a gym, and an auditorium with rooms for band and orchestra. SBHS had also expanded across a side street where a few hastily-flung-up, pre-fab bungalows housed foreign language classes, and across the alley, the journalism classroom and the print shop.

These latter two shared a connecting door, and their own unique smell: ink, metal, cheap paper, that classroom-yellow-chalk, and the whiff of cigarettes. The print shop teacher was a young guy whose face I can see, but whose last name eludes me, because everyone called him Phil. Phil smoked cigarettes, and he tolerated smoking from his guys. All the printers were guys. The journalism students were an odd mix, boys and girls, Black, white and Mexican. The journalism teacher, Mr. Sam Feldman, was an easygoing sort and more than one kid took his class because it was known you could get a decent grade from him if you loped along and did the minimum. Even the minimum, however, required a good deal of work because every Friday we published and distributed the *Tyro Weekly*. Four printed pages—covering student life, sports, the arts, the administration—that required interviewing, taking notes, writing, fact-checking, proofing, buying ads, doing the layout, including photographs, all overseen by Mr. Feldman, but the work done by the students. No small weekly feat.

Sam Feldman had started out as a sportswriter with a degree in journalism from the University of Southern California. Though he was physically ill-suited to sports—a short, doughy, roly-poly, jovial, cigar-smoking man—he loved going to games, talking sports, stats and scores. He told the story on himself that on his wedding night he took his bride to a basketball game. He also occasionally wrote for the sports page for the local rag, the *San Bernardino Sun-Telegram*. How he happened to come to SBHS to teach, I do not know. While he was there, the *Tyro Weekly* won many

Southern California journalism awards, and several editors of the *Tyro Weekly* walked into jobs at the *Sun-Telegram* shortly after high school.

Journalism was an elective for someone like me on the college-prep track. Academically SBHS was largely segregated with only a handful of Black and Mexican students in the college-prep classes. For the most part, white, Black and Mexican kids mingled in classes like PE, or Drivers' Ed, or band or art or journalism.

Journalism was my favorite class. Moreover, it was the first period, and I could come in late, as long as I appeared before the attendance slip had been picked up. Mr. Feldman always listened to my excuses with a bemused look. One day he even quit marking me late; he said he actually looked forward to what new excuse I would come up with. He liked my stories.

Mr. Feldman subscribed to the *New York Times* for classroom use, and as I read its long, prim columns, I dreamed of seeing my byline there. In the meantime, my byline appeared regularly the *Tyro Weekly*, and that too was a thrill. I turned in a story every week, often lengthy pieces that had to be researched or interviewed and written (there was a separate glassed-in space in the classroom with half a dozen huge typewriters lined up; the clattering was incessant and deafening). What did I write about? Lively profiles of math wizards, and drama students (Mollie Ryan, born for Broadway! Where are you now?). But the one I remember best was a long historical piece about the guy who had written the School Hymn in 1916. The melody and lyrics to the School Hymn still burble in the bilgewater of my brain.

"Hail Hail, SB High, All Hail to Thee!
Honored by many, cherished by all
Daughters and sons thy greatness exalt.
Noble in purpose, grand in thy might
All hail to thy sable and cardinal bright
Hail Hail SB High, All Hail to Thee!"

This School Hymn hung on a banner in the gym and was emblazoned elsewhere around the campus. So...I wondered, where did it come from? Who wrote it? I researched this, and I somehow found this guy, David Greenhood, and wrote to him. (He had long since left San Bernardino.) To my surprise, he wrote back. Mr. Greenhood had graduated in that first class of the "new" school, 1916, and he cordially answered my questions. Moreover, he added, he had actually written and published a novel, *Love in Dishevelment*. My mother thought this was a very racy title and wondered if this was actually a story I ought to pursue. She needn't have worried; I could not find the novel anywhere, not even in the city library, much less the school library. However, on Amazon.com to this day you can see its spicy 1949 Signet paperback cover: a disheveled couple, clearly about to jump into the Throes of Passion amid spilled wine glasses and yucky dirty ashtrays.

II

In my senior year I probably should have moved from features editor to editor-in-chief of the *Tyro Weekly*, but I didn't. That plum position went to Bill Ray, a student who, had never been in journalism class. My father was annoyed that I wasn't made editor, but I wasn't especially jealous of Bill Ray; I liked writing the feature pieces. How Mr. Feldman found Bill Ray or approached him, I don't know. Bill Ray had transferred to SBHS, from whence I do not know, and maybe he had journalism background there. He was a very odd duck. Tall, thin with broad shoulders a sharp, beaky nose, dark, rather wiry hair, a narrow mouth, and alert, darting eyes behind thick glasses. He was one of those people who must endure adolescence until they can get to where they really belong which is about age forty. In the beginning, I thought him No Fun At All, and indeed he wasn't. He smiled but he didn't often laugh. As far as I knew, he had no particular friends, and didn't seem to miss any. After I quit judging him by the No Fun At All standards, he was, in fact, an education to me, and we came to be good friends. I admired him. He was certainly the smartest person I had ever met (one of the smartest I've ever met). Of the four hundred graduates in our class, he swept all sorts of academic honors. At graduation he stood for pictures, solicitously, protectively beside his mother, his only family; Mrs. Ray looked oddly stunned, and behind her thick glasses her eyes seemed to wobble. Bill Ray, needless to say, did not go to work for the *Sun-Telegram* after graduation. He went on to Berkeley, and though I lost touch with him after a few years, I am happy to think of him there, riding high on the tide of the late Sixties activism and intensity.

Those two words, activism and intensity could have been his middle names. His first editorial in the high school student paper was a scathing condemnation of the weak US response to the Hungarian Revolution in 1956. Trust me, the Hungarian Revolution had never crossed my mind, not in 1956, not ever, until I read his column in the *Tyro Weekly*. And yet, Bill Ray's writing was so powerful, that now, decades later, I can recall his final line: "They asked for tanks, and we gave them chocolate bars." Who writes like that, with that kind of passion about a failed revolution in a foreign country in a high school newspaper? Especially in this, the era of *Animal House*, and *American Graffiti*? The school administration was very upset with this editorial criticizing the US government. Though I do not remember any particulars of the struggle (and perhaps I never knew the particulars) I knew that Sam Feldman stood by Bill Ray's right to publish it. Sam Feldman recognized that Bill Ray was brilliant, just as he recognized that I could spin a good yarn.

Mr. Feldman's classroom offered sanctuary to lots of oddball students who congregated there often at lunchtime. You didn't need to be as smart as Bill Ray to hang out there; you didn't even need to be a good writer; you just needed not to fit in anywhere else. (The drama room and the band room and the art room offered the same sort of oases for those kids.) From some of these kids I learned a great many phrases that would never have occurred to a middle class white girl like me. What it meant to "tennis shoe the bill," and to "hotfoot" and to "hoof it." I learned what it might mean to be a knocked up Black girl just trying to graduate before her baby was born. In the journalism classroom, and in writing about people outside my own immediate set of friends and tidy, untested values, I got little glimmers of humility and humanity.

III

Mr. Feldman gave me the start in "My Future Occupation." In my junior year I went to work on the "Teen Scene" for the local rag, the *Sun-Telegram*. I didn't audition or apply for the job. I just showed up one Wednesday night at his suggestion, and I was hired. Not exactly hired, I worked for free for at least a year, and then they started to pay me, ten dollars for the feature story each week. The "Teen Scene" appeared, every Friday, a full page, of local teen news and features. The editor of the "Teen Scene" was Marty Mullins, and though she accepted my help, she maintained, shall we say, a withering distance, and we were never friends. She barely tolerated me. I was in awe of her.

Marty Mullins was perhaps four or five years older than I. She was brassy and confident, even jaded, cosmopolitan. I feared her. Not that I feared she would she fire me (though I suppose she could have, at least after they started to pay me) but she could and did make me feel very stupid. (No one could say "stupid" like Marty Mullins; she formed the word in a peculiar way, as if she were sucking on it, and then puckered up to emphasize the "p.") When I told her I'd been accepted at UC Riverside, she looked genuinely surprised, and remarked that she thought only smart people got in there. Marty was tall, broad shouldered, big-boned with a sharp nose, straight brown hair, and piercing brown eyes.

Marty Mullins and her older sister Agnes were legends in the small world of San Bernardino journalism. Agnes was the elder, but my path never really crossed hers, so I only knew the legend. The Mullins girls were smart, good writers, high achievers, though neither went to college. The sisters had each been an editor of the *Tyro Weekly* in high school, and gone to work for the *Sun-Telegram* after graduating. (With perhaps a brief stint at the junior college.) At the *Sun-Telegram* the Mullins sisters acted as assistants to Miss Winifred Martin, editor of the Women's Pages. In the vast undifferentiated workspace that was the newsroom (save for the editor-in-chief's glassed-in cubicle) the Women's Pages were three desks pushed together in a windowless corner. Marty and Agnes faced each other; Miss Martin's desk with its single rose in a slender vase, was at the top. Miss Martin had been Women's Editor at the *Sun-Telegram* since the dawn of time.

Winifred Martin was the Hedda Hopper of San Bernardino. For forty-plus years she wielded unbelievable influence among the city's social elite. (An elite that, trust me, was reflected in the high school social order.) At the newspaper she reigned supreme in a world of Recipes and Events. Until about the 1970s the Women's Pages in American newspapers had not changed since the *Dinosaur Times*. Certainly when Marty and Agnes Mullins came to write for the Women's Pages, the content could still be described as I did below in my novel, *American Cookery*:

> *Women's Pages did not print articles about PMS, ADHD, STDs. They did not offer lead features about erectile dysfunction, or what to do if you found your son wearing women's clothes, or your husband cheating with a co-worker, or how to choose a therapist, or talk your daughter out of getting her bellybutton pierced. There were only two possibilities: Events and Recipes. Recipes were variations on canned soup, canned tuna and corn- flakes; dessert was anything with a maraschino cherry. As for Events, any delightful occasion dignified by the presence of the Editor of the Women's Pages became an Event. So unquestioned was this editor's autocracy that her gushing description of a reception for a couple who had "eloped" months before could bestow unquenchable respectability upon children who had been conceived in the backseats of cars.*

Winifred Martin, I later learned, had come to San Ber- nardino as a child in about 1900, from Kansas with her parents and brother. Her father was a newspaperman and he brought his press on the train with him, and set up in San Bernardino. Here the Martins' paper prospered, and like her father, Winifred loved working there, loved the smell of ink and metal, loved helping him print and write and proof, all those tasks associated with getting a newspaper into the hands of readers—never mind, and not caring that the next day that page goes at the bottom of the bird cage or is used to wrap fish. Her mother and brother did not love the newspaper business. When her father died, sometime in the early 1920's, her brother (who had married and left town) insisted on selling the paper and its lucrative list of subscribers and advertisers, to the fledgling *San Bernardino Sun*. Winifred fought this, but she could not run the paper herself. She gave in and sold, but not before extracting a promise that she would always have a job at the *Sun*, and they honored this.

I learned all this because in the 1990's—for reasons I still do not understand—Winifred Martin began to haunt me. So persistent was this skinny specter, intermittently begging to be known, that on one of my family's SoCal jaunts, I went to the San Bernardino public library where I put old microfilm of the *Sun-Telegram* on the machine, and spent the afternoon whirring through forty-plus years of her life, her columns, her feature stories, and her obituary. I left the library imagining her daily arrival at the *Sun-Telegram*, a thin woman stalking through cirrus clouds of cigarette smoke in the newsroom, past the men's desks, as though she were a gloved-and-hatted dingy navigating treacherous shallows. I imagine that the sportswriters and city desk men, the cop-beat writers and the wire service writers, even the copy editors treated her with sarcastic deference that masked their begrudging fear of her, and the fierce unswerving loyalty she commanded among the city's elite. I left the library wondering too, if every local rag had a Winifred Martin, some misguided old bat who actually thought she could write, who had the temerity to challenge the men in their newsroom citadel. I left the library believing she was both heroic and pathetic.

Miss Martin never married, never retired, and when she died the paper ran her picture (impossibly thin, heavy glasses, boot-black hair, always a hat and gloves) alongside a photograph of the typewriter on her empty desk, a single rose in a vase, her signature, so to speak. After her death the *Sun-Telegram* instituted an annual award, the Winifred Martin Award for Best Girl Journalist in the City. The year I graduated, 1962, I won the Winifred Martin Award (there were only two high schools, so it wasn't exactly competition for a Pulitzer). Presented to me by the corpulent, ruddy, Mr. Guthrie, publisher of the family-owned *Sun-Telegram*, the prize came with a pen-holder with a brass plaque, and a hundred dollars. This, along with the ten dollars they paid me for my "Teen Scene" stories comprised my first wages for writing—and my last until I sold my novel in 1977.

Marty Mullins wasn't impressed that I'd won the Winifred Martin Award. I cannot remember a single compliment from her for anything I wrote. I certainly would never have confided to her that I had dreams of writing for the *New York Times*. That said, UCR, where I went to college, had no journalism major, so I majored in history, and continued to work at the "Teen Scene."

Every Wednesday night for four years (two in high school and two in college) Marty Mullins, and I worked in that little corner of the newsroom allotted to the Women's

Pages amid the smell of ink of a hundred typewriter ribbons and the clatter of keyboards, and the ring and thrash of typewriter carriages banging back and forth. Well, perhaps not so much noise by the time I got there, around seven every Wednesday night. That late only the sportswriters were working in the newsroom. Sometimes Mr. Feldman showed up as well, and joined them. They were a raffish, affable bunch of middle-aged men, and though they were probably lecherous, they were harmless, and I liked hanging out with them. The building had air conditioning which meant there were no open windows, so the smoke (all the sports guys smoked; Marty smoked) collected and hung in the air. My job those four years was so lowly that when Marty and I finished, I took our copy down to the print room where there were crashing machines, the smell of ink and oil and metal, and cigarettes. Men, young and old with dirty hands, and big grins. No doubt lecherous too, but I didn't know the difference between a lech and someone who just thought I was cute. I was cute.

Like a wake fanning out behind a ship those "Teen Scene" Wednesday nights blend together in memory. What remained for me was the Wednesday Night Smell on walking into the building by the side entrance, the stairwell dividing the second floor newsroom from the basement print room. Of all those four years only two particular incidents stand out in memory.

One April, late in our association, Marty Mullins invited me to go to Balboa Island in Orange County with her, and the *Sun* photographer, Reggie Something for a "Teen Scene" story on Spring Break. All the cool (white) girls from San Bernardino went to Balboa Island for Spring Break. I was flattered and delighted to be asked, though I quickly came to understand that Marty brought me because she couldn't be bothered to take the notes, that is, to actually talk to the people we would quote when we went to the addresses where gaggles of cool girls were staying, chaperoned by their well-heeled mothers. I did the interviewing, checked the spelling on the names, and the like. Marty and Reggie ignored me on the way to Balboa, on the way back, and whenever possible in Balboa itself. I sat in the backseat listening to Marty bitch and heap shit on various people at the *Sun*, especially the higher-ups, including the owner, Mr. Guthrie.

The other vivid memory seemed to me validation of my dearest seventeen-year-old dreams. I came to work one Wednesday evening to find the Sun-Telegram building surrounded by wailing fire engines and a police cordon. The building right next door, an old furniture warehouse, was burning away. (I suspect arson for the insurance money; there was never anyone in it.) I pushed my way through to the police line and told them I worked at the *Sun*. I had no badge, no credentials, but they let me in! They believed me! Believed I was a reporter! To be up on the roof with Marty Mullins, and the *Sun* sportswriters, real reporters, soot and ash falling all around us, smoke swirling! To belong there! One among the wise-cracking, world-weary journalists. Heaven!

Also heaven: every Friday night I saw my name, my byline in a real newspaper, even if it wasn't the *New York Times*. My name atop a long column of glorious print! What did we publish in the "Teen Scene?" Features on all sorts of young (white) people and various groups from the two high schools in town, with occasional input from the Catholic school. Sometimes we even deigned to notice the activities of junior high students. There was a music column called "Platter Patter." Early on Marty fired the guy who wrote it. He was a jazz aficionado, and she fired him because he didn't write about music that her audience actually listened to. (However, I must say his column turned me on to Dave Bruebeck.) She hired instead the DJ from one of the two radio stations that played rock and roll. Shortly after I came to work there she also fired the girl who wrote a gossip column because this girl was twenty, and too old for it. Marty gave "Cruisin' Around." to me.

"Cruisin' Around" endowed me with more social power than I have ever had before or since. Enormous power. Winifred Martin power in the small hot world of high school San Bernardino. I had not beauty or athletic ability, the hallmarks of teenage celebrity, but every Friday, there was my byline atop the column, "Cruisin' Around," and thus, for that brief shining moment I lived at the hub of influence even though my close friends were not part of the In Crowd, and my family was not one of the social elite who lived on broad, leafy streets, or in homes with swimming pools. Moreover, I almost never went cruisin' around, thanks to my uber-strict Mormon father. So limited was my social life, for instance, that when I was actually given parental permission to go to a party after a school fundraiser spaghetti feed, I went, even though as the evening progressed, pain—that is, intestinal mortal agony—set in, food poisoning, as it turned out, tainted meat at the spaghetti feed. I never let on and I did not go home before my curfew.

The logo for "Cruisin' Around" was two pairs of eager-looking eyeballs, and the name came from the teenage pastime in that era (vividly portrayed in the film *American Graffiti*) of, well, cruising around in cars. These were motorized mating rituals. The cars had bench seats, and where the girl sat on that bench, her proximity to the driver, announced to the world the status of the relationship. The cruising didn't just happen on any old street. No. There were certain destinations, Mini-Meccas, where kids hung out, and there were certain routes to those destinations where on weekend nights long lines of cars, big cars, vehicular citadels of teenage pomp and power, drove slowly by, radios blaring often in unison because there were only two rock stations in town. These cars were mostly refurbished vehicles from the early fifties with rounded lines that had been re-fitted with tuck-and-roll upholstery, shiny hubcaps, and above all, deeply rumbling motors, so loud they sounded like a bass chorus. (A friend once told me she always chose to sit in the backseat because she could pleasurably feel the vibration of the motor all over her butt.) These cars were usually driven by guys, and if the driver didn't have his girlfriend beside him, then the car was filled up with other guys. Occasionally there were cars full of girls who at stoplights pulled up alongside these cars full of guys. Sometimes these cars of guys and cars of girls all got out and exchanged places. It was, in short, a world of rumbling cars and horny boys and girls who slid across the bench seat to sit thigh-by-thigh beside them

"Cruisin' Around" was like Twitter that happened once a week. Journalistically the *Tyro Weekly* dealt in facts, even the features dealt in facts. *The Sun-Telegram* dealt in facts, even the "Teen Scene" dealt in facts. But "Cruisin' Around" dealt in rumor and innuendo. Many ellipses leading to the next juicy bit with first and last names. . .who might have been doing what on Friday night. . . Who Was Seen With Whom??? And Where???? Of course there were code names for places where people were not supposed to be, like the closed-up hot springs in the hills above the city where reportedly there was skinny-dipping, or the Point, the "lookout" over greater, glorious San Bernardino where couples in cars went to neck and pet and beyond. Or certain people's houses where there were parties when the parents were away. I filled "Cruisin' Around" with the activities of my friends, naturally, lending them new cachet, but largely, since my actual social life was so seriously circumscribed, I filled it with what people told me. I broadened out beyond the cool kids even beyond the white kids, offering opinions often unwelcome. I took shit from more than one of my peers for remarking on the football achievements and the good looks of two Mexican brothers.

San Bernardino is still fondly known by those of us who grew up there as the Armpit of the Nation. There were sometimes gang fights on Saturday nights, guys with chains who would fight in parking lots, a la *West Side Story* while other teens would stand around to cheer and jeer. I never personally witnessed one of these, but they were the talk of the school on Mondays. San Bernardino was (and remains) much rougher, poorer, more economically, culturally and racially mixed than other nearby towns, genteel Riverside, artsy Redlands. White, Black and Mexican kids attended the elementary schools that served unofficially segregated neighborhoods, junior highs melded some of these neighborhoods, but SBHS drew students from the whole city. (Pacific High opened in the late 1950s.) The high schools brought everyone together. In a manner of speaking. Socially, students kept to their agreed-upon spaces in the cafeteria and the Quad. Entrance to that space had to be granted. This exclusivity was particularly, poignantly true for those elite, ethereal realms of the Truly Cool kids, white kids who wafted among us like beings from another world, radiating confidence we mere mortals couldn't even imagine, much less hope to emulate. To be asked to join High School High Society was like having a knighthood conferred.

Though Black and Mexican students outnumbered white kids by two to one (I'm guessing at this ratio; it might have been more) in this era prestige of any sort was strictly a province for white people. All the teachers and coaches and administrators were white, all the student body officers and cheerleaders and pom pom girls, etc. etc. (the aforementioned ethereal elite) were white. Sports, however, were integrated. Lots of Mexican and Black kids rose to high school superstardom on the football, basketball, track and tennis teams. High school football and basketball games called out massive, enthusiastic crowds, so much so that football games were held at the county fairgrounds, and basketball games packed the gym.

Sports met High School High Society at the homecoming festivities with their panoply of urgent questions to be asked and answered: who would be Sophomore Darling? Who would be Junior Darling? And who would be the Homecoming Queen? The Homecoming Queen had to be a senior, nominated by a member of the football team, or the basketball team, but the whole school voted for the winner who was announced some two weeks before the big game. The Queen and her court had their photographs taken, and were lauded in the pages of the *Tyro Weekly*, and the "Teen Scene" as well. At the Homecoming halftime the band played an uptempo "Hail Hail SB High......" while the pageant unfolded. The Sophomore Darling and Junior Darling (lovely, dewy girls, both of them) were given bouquets, walked along the red carpet to the dais to sit on either side of the Queen's throne. The Queen's princesses (runners up) came next, and they stood on either side of her throne. The Homecoming Queen, tears of joy gleaming on her pink cheeks, was escorted to her throne by none other than the student body president himself. Everyone applauded. The student body president presented the Queen with a bou-

quet of red roses and a kiss on the cheek. More applause.
More music.

Only this particular year, my senior year, not only did
the Black kids nominate a Black girl for basketball homecoming queen, but they voted in a bloc. They voted with
their sheer, overwhelming numbers, and they voted in
Joanne Dawson, the very first Black Homecoming Queen
in what felt like the history of the world. So momentous
was this win, this choice for Homecoming Queen, you'd
think the earth might have altered its axis. Her court con-
sisted of the Sophomore Darling, the Junior Darling, and
two runners-up, princesses.

After the lovely Joanne Dawson was announced as the
winner, and after the *Tyro Weekly* did a big, showy photo-
spread of her with her white-girl court—and without men-
tioning she was the first nonwhite Homecoming Queen in
the history of our particular universe—one question burned
on everybody's lips: would the student body president, Bob
Davis, would he kiss her? The student body president had
kissed the Homecoming Queen on the cheek since 1915,
since the dawn of time, right? Would Bob honor tradition?
Would he have to? Would he dare to? To kiss a Black girl
in front of the whole world? Kiss Joanne Dawson front
of Sandy Barker, his girlfriend, a lovely student council
member and Homecoming Princess? Poor Sandy having to
watch her boyfriend kiss a Black girl in front of the whole
world!! Among the Black kids I'm sure there was much of
the same thrashing going on, no doubt with less care for
Sandy Barker's tender feelings. How did they feel about a

white boy kissing Miss Dawson? I have no idea. One can only imagine what the teachers and the coaches and the administration thought. The outcome of the game was moot. The question was The Kiss. The question of The Kiss would never appear in the *Tyro Weekly*, and it much too hot for the "Teen Scene," or even "Cruisin' Around." But it burned through the school, and the stakes felt blisteringly high.

I was in the camp that believed Bob Davis (I have changed these names) ought to kiss Joanne Dawson; she was the Homecoming Queen and he was the student body president, and this was a tradition. But there were those, even among my friends, who firmly believed he could not and should not kiss a Black girl. It would be, well, unthinkable! One wonders what sort of counsel Bob Davis was getting from his teachers and parents. And what of his girlfriend? How to meet this immense challenge to their youthful love? Sandy Barker probably cried her eyes out while she and Bob parked at the Point, necking and petting.

On that infamous homecoming night, in February, 1962 the band played "Hail, Hail, SB High," as Bob Davis escorted the beautiful Joanne Dawson to her throne.

He gave her the roses.

He held out his hand, and with only a split second of hesitation, she took it. They shook hands.

The entire gym exhaled in one breath. Some in relief. Some disappointed. The applause was weird.

I have no idea what finally determined Bob Davis's decision to decorously offer his hand. I have no idea what Joanne thought. I didn't know Bob Davis or Joanne Dawson, and I don't know what became of either one of them after high school. But I have to wonder: does Bob Davis ever revisit that Homecoming night in memory? Perhaps in dreams. Does he return to that night, and wish he had done things differently? Does he ever think that if—maybe just if—he had chosen to kiss the beautiful Joanne Dawson, might his whole life have turned out differently? Might he have been a better, stronger man for having dared something so very dangerous in 1962?

All struggles are magnified for adolescents. As in *West Side Story*, the rifts and loyalties loom large, enormous in the mind and heart because kids have the passions, but not the context, because, though they do not know it, their world is so narrow: the tensions of home, school, a neighborhood, a job perhaps, the finite cast of characters, even stock characters: the jock, the popular girl, the Bad Boy, the frail kid picked on by the others, the musician, the pocket-protector math whiz, the girl who puts out for a lot of boys, the sheltered girl who kisses with her lips firmly pressed together. In memory these characters are frozen in their perceived poses, as though no one will ever grow or change. Their dramas linger long after the stock characters themselves have gone far away, have gone gray or bald, have gone deaf, have gone to fat or wasted away, have lost their sight or lost their marbles, lost their mobility, have died, their little lives rounded with a sleep.

IV

Life went on.

I graduated along with Bob Davis, Joanne Dawson, Bill Ray and four hundred others. I gave up "Cruisin' Around" when I went to UCR. The "Teen Scene" dropped it as a feature. Agnes Mullins got married. Naturally, the wedding got written up in the Women's Pages with Marty as a bridesmaid. By day Marty worked with her sister. Wednesday nights she worked with me. I brought in draft already typed up at seven pm; Marty would edit, making her changes, proofing, laying out the page, and a little after nine I would take our copy down to the print room while I still dreamed of my byline in the *New York Times*.

One Wednesday night some months after the Balboa trip, as we were wrapping up, Marty Mullins announced she was quitting the *Sun-Telegram*, leaving to take a job as a stewardess. I was speechless. Really, jaw-drop speechless. Marty preferred pouring coffee on airplanes to working for the newspaper? Being a stewardess was glamorous, yes; they wore slim skirts, high heels, often cute little caps; they were groomed to a brilliant polish and smiled nonstop. But Marty Mullins? She did not suffer fools gladly (as I knew from experience). I could not imagine her being charming. I don't remember what I said after I recovered my wits, but I certainly did not denigrate serving coffee on airplanes. I still feared her. I muttered something to the effect that I thought working for the newspaper was a dream-job. To this observation, Marty Mullins snorted. She said there was no future for women in journalism, not for any woman. Women would never be allowed to move beyond the Women's Pages, Recipes and Events. Maybe Agnes was fine with that, but Marty would not stick around to be one of those women who, in a phrase, eat mush and take shit.

If Marty Mullins, brassy, sassy, and smart, believed there was no future for a woman in journalism, if she felt compelled to leave the newspaper business, what could I possibly hope for? I had none of her steely panache. I quit the "Teen Scene" when she did. I gave up the hope of being a journalist when she did. I could never be Marty Mullins, but I did not want to be Winifred Martin either. Even if I was the Best Girl Journalist in the City.

Many years later I created a character, Eden Douglass, who shared my youthful journalism ambitions, though she lived in another era (b. 1920). Eden too started out as a kid in a lowly position working for a local rag writing obits. As a young woman, in 1946, she got a job (through nepotism) on the *St. Elmo Herald*. She was assistant to the Women's Editor, Winifred Merton. Eden was an uppity assistant, and during Miss Merton's enforced absence from the paper (due to food poisoning at an Event) Eden institutes what she thinks are innovative changes for the Women's Pages, content beyond Recipes and Events, content that reaches out beyond the city's Mormon and Methodist elite. Miss Merton, on her return to the newsroom, is not amused. Miss Merton, who has heretofore treated Eden with mere glacial disdain, erupts.

"*Get out of this newsroom, Miss Douglass! Get out of this business. Get out of this town. Do something, anything, but get the hell out of here! Now! Before you are tied to complacent people who will never regard you with anything but pity. Even contempt. Get out before you are tied, inextricably, to the smuggery you so clearly detest. Do you really think in a few years' time you'll have earned this paper's respect? Do you think you'll be over there, with them?*" She raised her boney finger and pointed to the men, the shirtsleeve brigade, wreathed in stale smoke. "*Perhaps ten year's time? Twenty? Do you think that in 1966 your byline will be atop a story that isn't a Recipe or Event?*" Miss Merton wheezed out a dry, unpracticed laugh. "*You are a fool, but surely you're not so foolish as that. Do you really think that you are so fine a writer, that your gifts will grant you a desk in the newsroom, that you will write for the world,*" she added, rasping and impassioned. "*Use your eyes! Look at me! Ink is in my veins, I tell you! I breathed newsprint from the day I was born. When my father brought the printing press to St. Elmo, we slept in the freight car with the press, that's how dedicated we were to the newspaper business. My father could set type so fast, his hands were a blur. He taught me my letters at age three so I could help him set type. I loved the sound of the press, and the clank of the type and the hot metal and the ink!*" Miss Merton was breathless now. She struck the desk with an impassioned fist. "*I was writing copy, setting type, when other girls were dressing up their dolls.*" She advanced on Eden, shouting. "And then my father died, and my worthless brother deserted me, and I had to close the Gazette. The owners of the Herald wanted my presses, and my list of subscribers, and I sold it to them. But only on the condition that I would work at the Herald. And I do. What a success story! Do you think it was my ambition to chronicle who went where and what they wore, and how lovely were the celery sticks and fruit punch, how Mr. and Mrs. Methodist are having a tea on Friday?" She gingerly plucked the dead rose from its vase and dropped it in the trash can. "Do you think I really give a damn?"

I have no idea what happened to Marty Mullins after she left the paper, despite the usual internet search. Perhaps she married a pilot and changed her name. If she did get married, she didn't announce her wedding in the *Sun-Telegram*; I have looked through their pages online and found her name nowhere after she left the paper. Whatever she did, even as a stewardess, she would have met life with her trademark cool condescension, the *sangfroid* I could never muster, much less master. Marty Mullins' choice to leave the newspaper was a loss to the world of journalism; she was an astute editor. Smart. Capable. A fearless and often tyrannical leader. For myself, I very much doubt I would have been one of those glamorous reporters with a byline in the *New York Times*. Rising to the challenges of being a woman in that male-dominated profession, that and much else would have defeated me. I would not have had the energy left over to know if I was any good as a writer.

Moreover, I like writing long paragraphs, loopy sentences, and sometimes swooping prose. I like to muse on, ruminate about what I put on the page, to edit, revise, return to it, rethink. I am intrigued with rumor, innuendo, with what can be distantly whispered, rather than introduced in a one sentence lead and verified by multiple sources willing to go on the record.

So perhaps it is altogether fitting that "My Future Occupation" became the career I could barely bring myself to say. As a novelist I have spent my professional life spinning yarns, writing thousands of "pages of ideas that just won't work on paper," honestly, probably millions of pages, stuff I threw in the trash can or recycled for the decades I worked on typewriters, the gizillion drafts rotting in the bowels of all the computers I have used, used up, and replaced, the many sad folders marked "Books Abandoned."

Sam Feldman gave me the only true writing class I ever had. From him I learned to love strong verbs, to avoid prepositions, and never to begin a sentence with "it." Simple directives that have served me to this day. And yet, I must admit that the first word in the first sentence in my first novel is "It." I thought long and hard about this "it," hearing his rules clanging in the back of my head. Still, I decided for all sorts of reasons, I had to open with "It was embarrassing from the beginning." I was prepared to defend my choice. When I published *Beggars and Choosers* in 1978 I telephoned San Bernardino High, asking if they might know how I might reach him, but Sam Feldman had left SBHS in 1963 or so, and no one had any idea where he might be, nor did the *Sun-Telegram* where all the old sportswriters I knew had died or retired.

A few years ago, perhaps in 2018 my mother saw Sam Feldman's name *In Memoriam* in the USC Alumni magazine. But when I hear thunder roll, I sometimes like to think it's the rumble of some heavenly press inking up his coverage of the angels' sporting events with his byline shining at the top.

CHAPTER FIVE

THE WAYWARD APPRENTICE

The past is a foreign country; they do things differently there.

> *~L. P. Hartley*
> *The Go-Between*
> *1961*

I

The day I was to have graduated with my master's degree in history from the University of Delaware, I was instead at the Philadelphia airport boarding a plane. I had scraped and saved all year from my paltry salary teaching English at a small college in Pennsylvania to fulfill a life-long dream of going to Europe, London, Edinburgh, Paris, Avignon, Nice, and on to a friend's house in Germany. The city I most wanted to see was Paris, the city of such ineffable romance that the very word wafted beauty, the city I had read about for years, the reason I took French in the first place. Once I was actually there, in Paris, what did I do? Clutching my dog-eared paperback copy of *The Letters of F. Scott Fitzgerald* I went to each of his addresses, like a ghost-groupie, and stood there, as if I could will myself through the windows and breathe air still scented with his prose. I went to the address where Gertrude Stein and Alice B. Toklas had held court for that coterie of almost unimaginable talent. I ordered a drink at the renowned bars where my literary heroes of the 1920s had hung out. I imagined them at nearby tables and myself part of this cadre of writers and artists I so admired. I walked into the legendary Shakespeare and Company bookstore, breathed in its aroma of fresh print, and dreamed that books I had written were on their shelves. In short, I imagined myself a fiction writer.

I did not, however, have the courage to write fiction, not since I was twelve when I scrawled some thirty or forty pages of a novel about the French Revolution. The heroine was—surprise!—a girl twelve years old. The manuscript romped along until realized that I knew no French other than "oui." I knew almost nothing of the French Revolution (save for *A Tale of Two Cities*) and very little about the eighteenth century in general, except that people wore difficult clothing and drank ale from tankards. Actually, I knew nothing of ale or tankards either. Perhaps, I thought, when the story spluttered, I should stick to just being a reader. And that's what I did for the next fifteen years.

The heroines I admired in the kids' books I loved, even the bratty heroines like nasty Mary Lennox in *The Secret*

Garden, had pluck, and a sturdy bravado. They were dashing, spirited girls whose exploits went persistently against the grain of feminine expectations; they repudiated the virtues for which girls were usually lauded, sweetness, propriety and the like. These many girls—rising up out of the pages of hundreds of titles I have long forgotten—made a tremendous, collective impression on me. I longed to repeat their adventures. I wanted to be a heroine, to travel, to go through the world with spirit and dash, and naturally, to be rewarded for my courage.

I read voraciously, ingesting these novels, and in a manner of speaking, coughing them back up. One afternoon after school my mother asked me to do something, and I replied, "Ooey."

"What?" asked my mom. "Ooey?"

"Yes, well that's what they say in this book I'm reading. It takes place in Que-beck, and that's what they say, Ooey"

My mother just shook her head and corrected my French.

Later she did more than correct my language when I called my little sister Helen a slut. I tried to explain I had read it in *Johnny Tremain* and that slut just meant someone messy. My mother was unconvinced.

I had memorized the whole first chapter of *Johnny Tremain*. Set in Boston just prior to the Revolutionary War, this Newberry Medal-winning novel tells the tale of an orphaned silversmith's apprentice unwillingly plunged into the cauldron of political unrest. The girl in the story, Cilla, is Johnny's friend, but mostly she listens and doesn't act. I wrote a letter to the author, Esther Forbes, suggesting that she write a sequel with Cilla as the central figure, the heroine. Miss Forbes gallantly replied, and though she had no intentions of a sequel, if she did write one, she would keep my suggestion in mind. *Johnny Tremain* was her only book for young readers so I checked out a couple of her other novels and read them too. I wondered what was so wrong about two people being in bed together in the middle of a Boston winter.

By the time I was twelve I had read all the novels in the kids section at the Reseda storefront library, but after my father was transferred to San Bernardino there were no more bi-weekly trips to the library. My mother could barely manage the stress of the move: new house, new neighborhood, new schools for the kids; my youngest brother was an infant, and my sister continued to have long bouts of chronic, unexplained ill health. Moreover, my father's territory was so huge it now included Las Vegas, and this meant that once a month he was gone for a whole week. Contributing my part to the general misery of those years, at thirteen I embarked on the long snotty stage of my existence, wretchedly unhappy, uprooted from all the friends I had known for what amounted to my entire life.

Amid all this upheaval, that first summer in San Bernardino the neighbor's sister died, and unexpectedly ameliorated the situation. She was an avid reader, and the neighbor gave her entire library to my mother, probably twenty-five years worth of basically Book of the Month Club titles. All through high school I read these novels (now with some better notion of what bed meant, Boston winter or no). From them I concocted new notions of what it meant to be a heroine which included, indeed, obliged the search for a hero who, like Cinderella's Prince, will validate her heroine-hood with marriage and true love.

Whatever may happen in novels, for the real-life heroine this search for a hero means wading into the murky swampland, the pith and plunder, the mulch and suction, splendor and grief of sex, guaranteed to keep her roiling for years. For myself, I thought true love was fine, and attractive. But marriage? Being beholden to someone else? Promising to be beholden? Not so attractive. However, being engaged was fun.

One of the young men to whom I was engaged (a perfectly nice person, and very handsome) urged me to elope with him when I was nineteen. We were sitting at coffee shop planning our elopement, and he asked me what was that strange look that crossed my face.

I blushed. "I was just thinking of all the books I was going to write."

He brightened, as if this were no problem at all, and offered, "I'll help you write them!"

While I'm sure he meant well, I did not elope with him then or ever.

II

Having returned from my European jaunt clutching the *Letters of F. Scott Fitzgerald*, I taught one more year at the school in Pennsylvania, and then, in 1972, I left the East Coast forever. I went to live in the post-hippie-haven beach town of Encinitas, California where my parents some years before had stuck a little vacation trailer with canvas-flapped room tacked on the side. I lived there by myself, but one weekend my teenage brother came to visit, and we went out with some of my friends for beer and pizza. When we returned to the trailer, my friends immediately crashed in the cots that were protected by the canvas room. The kitchen table could be made into a bed, and I fixed that up for my brother who had had both more beer and more pizza than was good for him. Seeing him settled, I went down the short aisle where there were two little beds that we called Ozzie and Harriet. My Leftist friend was already snoring in one, and I lay down in the other. In the middle of the night I heard my brother call out my name miserably. I took the few steps to the kitchen and quickly reached under the sink for the bucket that usually caught drips from the plumbing and put it by his bedside. Just in time. After I made my little brother as comfortable as I could under the circumstances with a cool cloth on his forehead, I turned on the light over the sink, and reached into the book rack by the door. The book I found at hand was A *Room of One's Own*.

I had bought A *Room of One's Own* probably the year before, but I had not been able to read past the grim prunes-and-custard-beginning. That night, however, I sat on the three-legged stool, and read it from cover to cover. Beer, pizza, barfing, the plumbing bucket, snoring, snuffling in a canvas-flapped trailer. Could anything have been further from the pristine confines of A *Room of One's Own* with its implied curtained window, neat desk, fountain pen and creamy foolscap paper?

The strength, the impact, the brutal clarity of the Great Virginia's reasoned presentation, the unfailingly even, un-ruffled tone as she flung out these truths, left me undone. Sometimes I had to come up from the pages just to catch my breath. In the midst of all else shattering and compel-ling, I came upon this revelation. To paraphrase: *If a Mar-tian read novels and drew its conclusions about our society from the reading of novels, that Martian would believe that women, heroines, were very important, crucial to society, that what they did was of significance. However, if this well-read Martian were to actually come to earth, it would find these notions utterly false, bewilderingly wrong, totally belied by everything it beheld.*

There lay the cruel discrepancy: from the time I was a child I had taken as gospel the novels that assured me that females, that is to say, heroines, were important. But in the real world, this was utterly untrue. In the real world men did the important things; women were much more likely to be handmaidens than heroines, relegated to the background, influencers perhaps, onlookers more likely. In her crisp Victorian-inflected diction the Great Virginia spoke to me: "At best, my dear, the grown-up heroine might provide a writer with inspiration for his book. She might offer strength, belief, and fortitude so that he could write it. She might be his muse. She might smile to see her name and some recognition in the dedication of that book, but she would not *write* that book. To be the heroine she need only be. To be the author, she must write."

I stopped reading only to wring out cold cloths for my brother's forehead, to put a shawl around my shoulders and socks on my feet as the early morning chill seeped up through the thin floor. Though the Great Virginia kept her passion at a metronomic beat, her prose cool and measured, by the time I heard the neighbor's rooster crowing at dawn, she had shaken me to my very foundations. Virginia Woolf unwound my imaginative fingers from the girlhood dream of being a heroine and put in my palm, folded my fist over the nubbly, dry kernel of being a writer which is to say, having the courage to actually write. *Okay, Self* (I more or less said) *you have a Smith-Corona, plug it in, and let's do this.*

Just before my return to California I had been accepted to grad school in the Literature Program at UCSD, a hotbed of the French Deconstructionist avant-garde. These professors valued The Text and did not give a damn for the story. They had what amounted to lip-curling contempt for the creation of character, for the richness and roll of language, much less (*tsk tsk*) the emotions that a writer could wreak on a reader. That fall as I took notes and read their tomes (or tried to), their flights of Structuralist fancy were, to me, dizzying, inducing headaches. I found their way of reading to be bloodless, juiceless; it did not allow for being swept up in beautiful language, or plunged into the lives of memorable characters whose fates and foibles and choices keep the reader glued to the page, and linger in the heart when the book is closed. I was very much an anomaly at UCSD, but I had only myself to blame. After all, I had not chosen the place for its meritorious faculty; I chose it because it was seventeen miles from Encinitas, and that was where I wanted to live. At UCSD, certainly at the beginning, I told no one among my peers and compatriots of my true ambition, to become a novelist. I would have been laughed right out of Jacques Derrida's derriere.

Every day that I did not have to be on campus, or working weekends at a high-end coffee store, I set out to seriously heed the Great Virginia. I turned on the Smith-Corona. I rolled the paper in. I took a deep breath and faced this conundrum: that I should be my own harshest critic so that I should be a good writer, and yet evade the despair that I would never be good, indeed that I would never be a writer at all.

I had moved by then to an apartment on Fourth Street. There was no Fifth Street in Encinitas. Across from this building were empty windswept bluffs with a two hundred foot drop to the beach. My actual apartment, however, faced east, and offered only a view of the alley below us, and beyond that, the town. I shared this apartment with a man (not the snoring Leftist) who came with his own challenges, true, but they were, so to speak, in-house. Jay McCreary and I had met back East, both been teachers at the college in Pennsylvania. When our contracts there ended we quite separately came to UCSD as grad students, me to the literature program, Jay to Scripps Institute of Oceanography. In addition to his scientific pursuits, Jay was a serious student of the classical guitar; he practiced nonstop, and his music rang out of our sliding glass door so beautifully that sometimes people would stand in the alley just to listen.

III

For literary women of the 1970s the task was that of salvage. Scholars, students, readers, writers, and thinkers plowed, slogged and flogged through centuries of creative and political oppression, sexual and social repression to find gems of female expression that could be held up to the light and admired. Among that era's great literary treasures were Sylvia Plath's *The Bell Jar* (1963) and the re-discovery of Kate Chopin's *The Awakening* (1899). They were accorded a sort of instant canonization and appeared everywhere on the reading lists of survey lit classes, like the one taught by the young male professor where I served as TA.

The young professor began with Kate Chopin's *The Awakening*. As he offered his introduction, I was troubled by the implications. I finally raised my hand: *Look, don't you find it awkward, I mean, really, how are we to understand a book called The Awakening that ends with a suicide? Doesn't that imply that if a woman has the bad luck to be awakened, then the knowledge—creative or sexual or whatever—cannot possibly be expressed and finally it will kill her?*

The young professor smiled at me soberly. He said I had missed the point of this wonderful novel, that society had demanded the heroine's life *because* she'd been awakened.

This did not answer my question. I remained un-dazzled.

After *The Awakening* he assigned Sylvia Plath's *The Bell Jar*. Again, my enthusiasm was tempered by his opening remarks. He dutifully (and it was obligatory in those days) waxed on about the doleful fate of Creative Women, and in a larger sense, the really wretched fate of Creativity In Women. *Poor Sylvia. So sensitive, so creative, so talented, so deep and feeling and articulate. Look how society devalued, ran her down and plowed her under. Madness is the sole and only sane choice in the face of such negation and destruction. What else could she do, poor Sylvia but stick her head in the oven and turn on the gas, as though she were some poetic cake to be done to perfection?*

Not a dry eye in the house. But given my secret situation, flailing away on the Smith-Corona, I was filled not so much with sympathy, but with dread. Sylvia's education (Smith College and Newnham College, Cambridge) was stellar, the literary equivalent of credentials from the Julliard School of Music. My own background more closely resembled the lyrics of Chuck Berry's "Johnny B. Goode." Sylvia had early publication and applause. For my efforts I had nothing to show but rejection. If with all that, Sylvia Plath could be destroyed and defeated, what hope had I of becoming a writer? I wasn't nearly as creative or well-connected as she was, and even if I had been, well, to prove I was sensitive and artistic, must I, of necessity crack up, break down, court madness, flirt with suicide, sleep with death?

As I finished reading *The Bell Jar*, chills and nausea accosted me, physical as a hangover, the pain promised women who want to write and to think and to feel and create and achieve. I dropped *The Bell Jar* to the floor, and went into the spare bedroom where I found the Smith-

Corona humming. I turned it off. I stared at the drafts all around me: the twisted, disfigured, fatuous, disgusting draft of everything I'd tried to teach myself. I wanted to shred it all and cry. But I did not. Instead I opted for a truly futile gesture. I went back in the livingroom, picked up *The Bell Jar*, stepped out on the balcony of the apartment, and flung that book across the alley, watched it sail, gloriously aloft, and fall finally with a soft plop on the roof of the neighbor's garage.

If this were a novel, it would be lovely and dramatic to say I went right back in, turned on the typewriter and wrote deathless prose, but memoir aspires to truth, and the truth is I did not write again till I had led—in a sort of half-hearted, even half-assed way—the undergraduates' discussion group on *The Bell Jar*. I had to wash off, or take off whatever it was that infected Sylvia. I had to be able to say to her and all the Hallelujah Chorus of misery, those ghostly voices weeping in their spirit-beer: *I'm really sorry for what happened to you, but if I want to trek and smash through experience using a pen as a weapon, don't tell me I can't do it just because I'm a woman. If I'm not any good as a writer, that's one thing. But don't tell me that to be a woman and a writer, to be creative and achieve, to be creative and even want to achieve will doom me to failure and madness and destruction.*

As a grad student in literature I faked textual orgasm as best I could. Like all students in this program I was obliged to declare official topics—an author, a genre and an era—for my oral exams. If you passed these exams, qualifiers they called them, you moved into the PhD program. If you failed, you were shit out of luck. I persistently evaded the qualifying exams, especially after one professor had scrawled cryptically, even ominously across one of my papers that I had "too much imagination." As a grad student (and inasmuch as was possible) I took classes that would not require that I read *Wuthering Heights* as Marxian dialectic. I cajoled a couple of professors to do independent studies with me; these let me roam around in authors who appealed to me, reading voraciously in memoirs, in writers of the World War I era, in Dickens and the nineteenth century (these were the genre, era and author I had chosen). I took classes from visiting profs who wouldn't be sitting on qualifying exam boards because they would be gone.

The most memorable of these was the poet Ed Dorn who came for one term, offered a class in Literature of the West. Great! Mark Twain, Mary Austin, John Steinbeck, Edward Abbey, right? That very first night Dorn (a thin man with gray, sun-strained eyes, a shock of gray curly hair atop a face lined with creases) did not take attendance, or hand out a tidy syllabus. No. He unfurled a huge sheaf of maps across the seminar table, and kept shaking his head, pointing at them randomly, and saying, "Will you look at that? Will you look at that?" Half the class bolted after that night. The rest of us stayed entertained and perplexed the whole term. Other than Dorn and his maps, the class I best remember was a Whitman seminar taught by an elderly, semi-inebriate prof. Whitman, with his sloth and splash, his ease, his large embrace and elastic ego ("I contain multitudes!") did not endear himself to the Structuralists, but I quite loved him. I wrote a paper called *The Lonesome Highway: Conversations between Jack Kerouac and Walt Whitman in the Afterlife* which I later turned into a story. This prof called it "a thing of beauty."

As for the teaching, I left Literature to the Structuralists and joined the Freshman Comp team of TAs. Even for a lowly freshman essay, there's only one central question: what makes good writing. That was the question I wanted to ask. And answer.

I V

As an apprentice writer I thrashed about on the Smith-Corona for three or four years, often in despair wondering what to write. I had no warm, well-known, beloved enclave from which I could draw character and inspiration. I had no ethnic or religious set of assumptions I could mine creatively for situations, dilemmas. There were no verdant hills, no rolling river, no rich cultural traditions to inform my work, to draw on. What could I possibly take from White Bread Eden and the Armpit of the Nation that would inform or infuse a work of fiction? Where to begin?

Well, what about my Master's thesis in history? No, don't guffaw! *"'An Ocean of Iniquity'": The Medical Department of the Continental Army 1775-1781."* was a great story! I was drawn to the project in the first place because of the great characters, vain, egotistical ambitious men with outsized personalities and equally outsized flaws—and a dramatic three-way power struggle among the founders of American medical education, culminating in a vindictive court-martial in wartime. But trying to turn it into a novel, I found I could not make the characters talk. Their dialogue as I rendered it correctly for their era was so stilted on the page they sounded like they had poles up their butts. Having written the word "lucky," I paused. In all my eighteenth century reading, I had never seen the word "lucky." I put the whole thing aside. Perhaps I ought not to attempt a long narrative.

I thought of my grandmother's Three Stories: the Cup of Coffee story, the Hot Water Tap story, and the Dumbbell story, those three charming stories plucked from the otherwise airless deep to which my grandparents consigned their past. She told and re-told each of these three stories in exactly the same way. Though I am ashamed to admit as much now, I thought cheerfully, well, at least I do not have to make them up! The stories are there! I just have to put them on paper!

As soon as I rolled the paper into the Smith-Corona and renamed the Cup of Coffee Story *A Child of Our Times*, that bubble burst. No way could I put myself into the mind, the heart and situation of a sixteen-year-old Armenian orphan living in a missionary school in southeastern Turkey in 1917—even if she was my own grandmother. I situated the story in the point of view of the school principal, Miss Towner, the American protestant educator whose name I changed. Many drafts later, pleased with the story, I gave it to my mom to type. I signed a manuscript with a loving inscription for my grandmother, certain she'd be pleased to see how I had reshaped her story, and look! There was her name, *Kalpakian*, on the title page! (I took this name, by the way, without asking anyone's permission, an act as I now see as unthinking usurpation). My mother gave my grandmother the manuscript when she went to LA to visit. My grandmother read it while my mother did the lunch dishes.

My grandmother was definitely not pleased. She scolded my mom, demanding to know why should I want to go back and revisit that awful old past? I was a young woman! An American young woman! I had so much before me! What was the point of writing about all this long ago misery?

Not until my mother was leaving, saying goodbye, did my grandmother add, "You tell her it was a glass pitcher."

"What?" said my mother.

"She wrote about a copper pitcher. You tell her it was glass."

This comment has always struck me as emblematic of my grandmother: even if she didn't like the idea, she would insist on the execution being done correctly.

The other two of her Three Stories, *Reunion* and *The Land of Lucky Strike* are immigrants' tales set in Los Angeles, and so easier to evoke. In writing each I discovered an abyss of pain I had never guessed at. With *A Child of Our Times* I also uncovered the abyss of my own ignorance. I published all three, and eventually reprinted *Reunion* and *The Land of Lucky Strike*. My grandmother never spoke to me personally about any of them, never validated nor denied the emotions I had grafted on to characters whose experience echoed hers, never offered another word of correction or praise or censure beyond the glass pitcher.

In these years I wrote all sorts of stories, some culled from scraps of tales, anecdotes told by others, stories ignited by sometimes ungovernable empathy. Some were fashioned from shards, the visible tips of the icebergs of my own life. Some, wholly imagined, created from what-ifs that rattled around in my head like unsecured cargo in a storm-tossed ship. For instance, the story of a working class girl, Kitty Tindall, in 1911 Liverpool who lives with a drunken mother and a heavy-handed stepfather. Literacy allows Kitty to feed her vivid imagination with dashing heroes, lovelorn heroines, and grandiose dreams of a career in the music halls. One day on her way to work, she happens on a Mormon tract left by missionaries. Smitten with the drama implicit in their account of the new gospel, and happy to raise her lovely voice singing hymns, Kitty converts. For such a girl (burgeoning sexuality, no particular allegiance to the truth) what might ensue? I worked on this story for a long time, off and on, calling it, *These Latter Days*, but even though it was never quite finished, it grew to an unwieldy thirty pages. The more literary fictions, like *The Lonesome Highway: Conversations between Jack Kerouac and Walt Whitman in the Afterlife*, (refined, revised many times and polished to a high gloss) these I sent to the prestigious literary quarterlies with university affiliations. I sent the many domestic fiction pieces to the major women's magazines that flourished in those halcyon long ago days when *Redbook, Good Housekeeping, Ms Magazine, Cosmopolitan, McCalls* published sometimes two stories a month. All my work was rejected.

One of my domestic fiction pieces I slid into a manila envelope and took with me to a conference or a program or some such Writerly Do that UCSD was hosting one summer. The main speaker on the first full day was the fiction editor of *Redbook*. I could not afford the couple of hundred they were asking to attend, but I showed up just the same. I didn't have a name tag like everyone else, but I filed into the lecture hall with the rest of the crowd, got a coffee and a doughnut just as if I belonged, and went way up to the top of the amphitheatre seating to the most obscure, unobtrusive place I could find.

The *Redbook* editor, Anne M. Smith, was a woman perhaps forty with a mild manner who gave a mild but encouraging speech. After the applause I watched as she climbed all the way up to the top tier of the amphitheatre and sat down beside me. Heart thudding, I waited till the next speaker finished, and then I turned and introduced myself to her and handed her the envelope with my story.

"Is this for the conference?" she asked.

"No," I said. "I'm a grad student, I can't afford the conference. It's for the magazine."

I thought surely she'll just hand it back. But she didn't. She slid it in her briefcase and descended the steps to be enveloped by crowds with questions and introductions. Me, I went home, delirious with possibility. Just imagine!

What a great tale I would have to tell about my first published story!

Later she mailed this story back to me with the tart editorial observation, "We think the wife has overreacted." I sent her many stories after that, and she usually returned them with comment, but she never published any of them.

At least she returned it with *Redbook* paying the postage. Being an apprentice writer would cost you a fortune in those days because with every submission, you had to include a Self-Addressed-Stamped-Envelope so your story could be rejected and returned to you at your own expense. Mine all were. For a time I kept these rejection notices pinned to the wall to prove to myself I was a serious writer. They became so numerous they depressed the shit out of me. I could not be immune from rejection, but I did develop a tactic to deal with the ongoing pain. I made it a practice to have out for consideration at any given time, at least three pieces. This meant when one came back, immediately another would go out. This way I could console, cajole, or simply happily lie to myself that surely the next editor would not be so stupid as to reject my beautiful work. It was, one might say, a game of literary/emotional hopscotch.

When even this strategy failed to insulate me from despair, I wondered if really, I just wasn't any good as a writer. I needed a real assessment, a truthful assessment, not just editorial rejection. I sent a copy of an ambitious story to Libby Nybakken, a dear friend from my University of Delaware days, and asked her to give it to a mutual friend, a young professor in the English department there. His short fiction appeared often in prestigious quarterlies, and I had read and admired some of his stories. I knew him in a glancing fashion, from parties at Libby's house, but enough that I did not want our acquaintance to color his judgment. I sent my story without any name on it, and asked Libby not to tell him who wrote it. Just the work itself, that's what I wanted him to judge. Generously, he read and returned my story to Libby, and she sent it back to me. His remarks were encouraging, though measured. Primarily, he noted the material bulged out of the story form. I could see he was right, but the story was so dense and daunting I had no idea how to approach it as a longer narrative. I put it aside, not returning to it until 2009. By 2010 it was a novel. I revised (off and on) for ten years. It remains the most ambitious book I have ever written. I am still revising.

A few of these early short fictions I published later, in magazines and literary journals, some in my first collection, *Fair Augusto and Other Stories* (1987). But most never appeared in print. When I stumble on these old drafts now and then, I cringe—not to think I could have written them (any writer begins with stuff that searches, gropes, flops and founders)—but that I could have sent them out believing them to be finished and fine.

After some three years of fruitless, that is, print-less writing, I got a letter, an actual letter, from *Ms Magazine* that they liked my story *The Great Jewel*, a fictionalized chronicle of how I parted with my virginity. *Ms Magazine* wanted to publish it in an issue they were planning on virginity. However, they wanted to publish it as memoir. My mother was aghast! Memoir meant that it had really happened! (I think she was imagining my grandmother reading it.) Me, I was delighted, never mind my grandmother. I replied with a resounding Yes! to *Ms Magazine*. Memoir it was! O Happy Validation! Take that, you withered followers of Foucault! I would be published in *Ms*! A few weeks later *Ms* returned *The Great Jewel* to me in my own SASE. Sorry. This rejection arrived on my birthday. I took it across the street to the bluffs, tore it into little shreds and let them drift down to the all-forgiving beach at high tide.

V

One June evening Jay and I were invited to a dinner party at the home of a visiting professor of French literature. I had taken his class, and he and his young family also lived in Encinitas; we had struck up a friendship because he too played serious classical guitar. Jay and I were the only grad students present at this dinner party; the other guests were younger faculty (including the prof enamored of *The Bell Jar* and *The Awakening*). But the guest of honor was without doubt, an august, elder-statesman professor, a silver-haired Spanish Lit critter of vast repute. He was renowned too for his enormous charm which he waxed on anyone within range, but especially attractive young women, and I happened to be seated beside him.

In his enchanting accent he regaled me with a fine, sonorous story of his exuberant youth in Spain: how he and his literary friend were devoted to poetry, their youthful travels while they wrote and dreamed of being Great Spanish Poets, of reviving the dreams of the Generation of '98, their hopes to sing Spain's Soul, and capture the essence of its people in immortal lyric verse. "But then," he added with a sad, expressive smile, "one day I realized I would never be anything but a Grade B poet, and that I could become a Grade A literary critic, and so I returned to the university."

He was certainly a Grade A critic; the whole world knew that.

I asked, "What happened to your friend?"

His bon vivant expression soured, but his features suggested a touch of contempt mixed with envy. He replied, "He is still a Grade B poet."

I said merely, "Ah." But I thought to myself: *Your friend is still a poet; he stayed true to the dream while you did not.*

I started the book the next day, though I did not know it would be a book, the story of a connection between a despairing, suicidal poet and a successful, smug English professor. When I reached page one hundred (with a ten-page parenthesis) I had to admit this was a novel with a subplot. Could I carry a long narrative in my head? Time to find out. I worked nonstop all summer on the novel I called *Then Beggars Would Ride*. (From the old adage, "If wishes were horses, then beggars would ride.") The story spilled out, with the central character dead from the beginning; it boasted a bevy of other, lively, interconnected characters, all of them struggling against the lunar tug of the past. Every day the material rewarded me with its energy, indeed what seemed to me the characters' own eagerness to become words on the page. I was riding the crest of a great creative wave.

Imbued with new confidence, when I saw an ad for the Squaw Valley Writer's Conference, in the *Los Angeles Times Book Review*, I applied. I submitted *The Lonesome Highway: Conversations between Jack Kerouac and Walt Whitman in the Afterlife*, and I was accepted! I only had to scrape together the considerable fee and the money for transportation up to northern California. I would meet other writers! I would get professional insight into my work! A heady prospect for someone who had always scribbled in secret.

Summer writers' conferences are ubiquitous now, but Squaw Valley, in the mountains near Lake Tahoe, was one of the earliest and among the most renowned. There were perhaps two hundred of us that year, aspiring writers of all sorts, poets, novelists, short story writers. Squaw Valley was a skiing destination, and they put us up in the dormitories, male and female, where the resort help was housed in winter. We were bunked by surname, and three of us, women whose names started with "K," stayed friends for years. We all laughed to think that none of us was using our legal names or we might never have met!

Afternoons for the six days of the Squaw Valley Writer's Conference were reserved for readings, panels and the like. Mornings were allotted to seminars where the work you had submitted was discussed in a session led by a faculty member. The main faculty were three men who had founded the Squaw Valley Writer's Conference perhaps ten years before. They had built homes here where they could retreat each day, and where they came in winter to ski. I'm going to call them Gent #1, Gent#2 and Gent#3,

middle-aged men with an impressive string of writing cred-
its, well-known names who also had university posts in
MFA programs. (This was the first time I had ever heard
of an MFA program.) Apparently there was to be a Gent #4
but he could not come, and so Gents #1, 2 and 3 invited the
San Francisco short story writer, Gina Berriault to take his
place. She too was middle aged, her dark hair streaked with
gray, slender, soft-spoken, intense. Though she certainly
wasn't bunked with us in the dorms, Gina took her meals
in the huge dining hall among the writers while the other
faculty retreated to their chalets.

For the sessions where individual work was considered,
your submission was duplicated and a copy given to the
faculty member, and each of the, say, fifteen or twenty
people in your group. These groups met in seminar rooms
at the resort. My experience teaching Freshman Comp had
endowed me with enviable skills and insights. I knew how
to read well, and I read the work of many, not just people
in the story session where *The Lonesome Highway* would be
discussed. Morning sessions were staggered, and there were
no limits to the number you could attend if you wanted
to, so I went to as many novel sessions as I could. As I sat
through these classes, I was dismayed to see some of the
faculty treat the aspiring writers with less respect than a
TA would give to a freshman essayist. Gent #2, for instance
approached a sci-fi novel in a particularly cavalier fashion.
It was written by a guy who looked like a kid to me, maybe
twenty years old; the material needed work, but it wasn't
hopeless. As Gent #2 offered his vapid opinions, he puffed

wisely on his pipe, and finally he turned to the kid and said, "XXXXX, I don't think you really believe in this book." The young man agreed he didn't believe in his book.

I wanted to slap Gent #2! How dare he say that? Of course this kid believes in his book! Why do you think he's coughed up his money, and is bunked here for a week with a bunch of strangers? He wouldn't be here if he didn't believe in it! None of us would!

Worse lay ahead. Gent #3 led the Story group I was part of where *The Lonesome Highway*: would be discussed on the third day. For the two days prior Gent #3 had led competent though not inspiring discussion, none of it especially fulsome, but none of it brutal, and some actually insightful. The writers in the group too, were lively, good readers. On that third day Gent #3 opened with *The Lonesome Highway: Conversations between Jack Kerouac and Walt Whitman in the Afterlife*. "Has anyone tried to write a story like this?" he began, grimly serious. "Two mythological characters assessing their lives after death?" He looked up and down the seminar table. Silence greeted this inquiry. Satisfied, he went on, "Well I have, and I can tell you, it just doesn't work, and this doesn't work. This story is stagnant, pretentious and boring. I ask you, why would anyone want to read it?" Anyone who tried to speak in defense of *The Lonesome Highway* was shot down, and anyone who wanted to join in the chorus of (basically) *shit shit shit*, got called on, and rewarded with beaming smiles and wise nods from Gent #3.

I was certain that everyone could see my blood, sweat and tears pooling on the floor under my chair. If I had had a car, I would have walked out of that room, and driven down the mountainside. Right then. But I did not. Like a surgical patient going under insufficient anesthetic, I could only concentrate on the pain as my work was eviscerated. He ripped *The Lonesome Highway* the proverbial new asshole, reviling the idea, savaging the execution, heaping abuse on the arrogance (who was I to put words in the phantom mouths of these immortals?). I had never shown my work to anyone except editors who rejected it (which, you couldn't take that personally) and here, my first time out in the world, I was told the story I had proudly polished to perfection was a not only worthless, but stupid, that my writing was fatuous and silly, and the very idea stank of derivative nonsense.

Many years later watching the *Great British Bake Off* and seeing those poor bakers being told that their conception was all wrong and their execution had failed and the texture was awful and the taste even worse, brought the whole Squalid Valley experience back to me like a quick slap upside the head. *Thank you*, the bakers always say after they've had their meringues forever flattened. Did I say *Thank you* to Gent #3? I have no recollection.

The following day Gent #3 had some other engagement and so Gina Berriault substituted for him, and ran our Story session, where she presided with gravity and courtesy and a genuine wish to help these writers understand their strengths and weaknesses. Inwardly I whined: *Why couldn't Gina have been the one to do my story?* I also noticed that in the afternoons when the dining hall was basically used as a study hall, Gina would find a quiet corner and work privately with the writers whose work had been dealt with in her seminars.

All right, I thought to myself, I have no car, I can't flee, and the worst has already happened. I might as well see it through to the end. I had also brought with me the thirty pages of *These Latter Days* about the 1911 Liverpool lass who takes up with the Mormons. I approached Gina Berriault and told her I knew I hadn't actually been one of her students, and I knew this piece was long, and I knew this-and-that-and-the-many-other reasons she probably could not get to it, but if she had the time. . . She said she would try. I could ask no more. I genuinely thanked her.

The last few days of the Squalid Valley Writers' Conference passed in a blur for me. I remained basically the walking wounded, the more stung because my humiliation at the hands of Gent #3 was so public that word of it percolated among the other writers, many of whom came up to me to offer condolences. I kept hoping that Gina Berriault would say to me, "Let's meet after lunch and talk about your story. . ." that she would take me aside as she had the others, talk to me, guide me through whatever could (or could not) be done with my story, but she never did.

On the very last day, everyone getting ready to go their separate ways, Gina Berriault came up to me in a crowded hall. She put the envelope with *These Latter Days* back in my hands. She said, "The only thing wrong with this is that it's not a story. It's a novel."

"Oh no," I clarified, "I'm already working on a novel."

"Well then, this is your second novel. I'm telling you, it's not a story. There's a novel here."

"Then you think it's....okay?" This last limp word was all I could eke out in lieu of *you don't think it's shit?*

The serious Miss Berriault gave me a wisp of a smile. "There's a lot of smart people here, but you have imagination. You have . . ." whatever else she said got drowned out amid myriad other voices, and she was called away, but before she left she said, "I've written my address on your envelope. If I can ever be of any help to you, let me know."

I was so buoyed by her words, I almost cried on the spot. But I still so shattered at the end of the conference that I have no recollection how I got down from the mountains and to the San Jose home of UCR friends. Once there, I slept for some sixteen hours. Only then, talking with them, could I face the implications of what had happened to me at Squalid Valley. If, truly, my writing was vain, fatuous, stupid and stale, should I not give up writing altogether, take my mother's advice, and get a teaching credential, a sensible American car, and a job with health benefits and a retirement plan? My longtime friend was vehement, "Fuck no! You don't have to believe that asshole!"

By the time I got back home to Encinitas, I thought, it's true that I actually have a choice here. I can believe Gent # 3, and part with my hopes and dreams, my now three-or-four year quest and efforts to write and publish, or I can say fuck you, you asshole, I am a good writer, and I'm going to finish this novel and prove it.

I told all this to Jay, and he too was indignant on my behalf. He knew how hard I worked at writing, just as he worked very hard at the classical guitar. Then I told him: if I can take fall quarter off from teaching and coursework, if I write full time for a few more months, I can finish the book. He agreed to float us for fall quarter on his research assistant's salary so I could stay home and write. I have been forever grateful for his generosity.

I took a leave of absence at UCSD, putting forth the fiction that I was studying for my oral exams. Then I stayed home and wrote fiction, often for eighteen hour days. I wrote and rewrote and revised again *Then Beggars Would Ride*. As the stack of "finished" pages mounted up on the right side of the typewriter, I grew increasingly neurotic, fearful of losing what I had written. What if there was a fire? What if there *was* a burglary? I nearly had a heart attack one night in December when we returned home and there was a burglary. Just like Ringo Starr said, they came in through the bathroom window, and they took the TV and the stereo, my grandfather's pocket watch and a pair of garnet earrings, but—thank you, Jesus!—they left the typewriter and the manuscript untouched. I wept with relief to see them still on the desk.

After that, each night when I went to bed I placed the "finished" portion of the manuscript in a tote bag. I placed the tote bag by the front door so that if there was a fire, I would grab it on my way out the door. (Not surprisingly, since I was a literature grad student, *Beggars* takes place largely in a university library, and one of the major characters is a meek, meticulous, hapless grad student, Grover Lerchke. Grover wraps his dissertation in foil every night and places it in the freezer in case there is a fire. Write what you know.)

In January I gave the finished *Then Beggars Would Ride* to my mother, the artist at the typewriter keyboard, to turn into a gorgeous manuscript. I returned to UCSD to take classes and teach Freshman Comp. So confident was I of the worth of what I had done, I announced to the other grad students that I had not studied for my exams, after all: I had written a novel! *Tsk tsk*, they scoffed, chiding me for the word novel rather than a text.

If this were fiction, I would surely leave my description there: moi, sashaying back among the Bloodless Structuralists, wonderfully confident in my work. But memoir aspires to truth. Truthfully, that confidence quickly eroded. Scuffling doubts, like rats-in-the-walls, kept me awake at night. *What about those oral exams, smart-ass?* Thus far in the literature program, I had laid low, teaching Freshman Comp, reading lavishly, but independently. In my wayward fashion, I had simply taken Incompletes in many classes; I never wrote the final papers so I could spend time on my own fiction. Those incompletes, seven of them, had to be finished within a certain time period, or they turned to F's. *If I'm not validated as a writer, not published, if I can't finish the incompletes, if I fail the exams. . ? What lies ahead? What would I be? Who would I be?*

I dutifully began the academic papers to remedy the Incompletes, but I also wrote query letters to perhaps twenty of the biggest houses in publishing. Replies drifted in, form letters and post cards that included the phrase, "We are not responsible for any loss or..." and so on. No names. Then, there came an actual letter, signed by an actual assistant on actual cream-colored embossed letterhead from Little, Brown in Boston. "We would be delighted to read your novel."

Done! I sent *Then Beggars Would Ride* to Boston on Valentine's Day. In the meantime I wrote to Gina Berriault and she helped me find an independent New York agent, a woman who had been in publishing for eons, who had started as an editor at Viking and had known John Steinbeck. This connection to my mother's best-beloved author seemed a good omen. We waited.

Mid-May I was given one of those rare moments vouchsafed to few when life meets art in a sort of Hallelujah Chorus of Harmonic Convergence. Indeed, the moment was like something you'd read in a novel. The powerful editor-in-chief at Little, Brown adored *Beggars*; he bought it outright for what felt like riches! Then he upped the price by two grand! More riches! On the strength of that golden moment, the money, the sunny prospects for success implied for all my glorious future, at the end of that spring term, (and ignoring everyone's advice) I sashayed out of graduate school, leaving seven Incompletes on my record, and never going near the oral exams. I waved *bye-bye* to the Deconstructionists, and declared myself a novelist.

A week or so later, renewing my passport (I had a Venetian friend who said, come to Venice and stay for a month!)

where they asked for my occupation, I wrote *Author/Novelist*.

I thought I would die of the happiness.

High tide! The events of that summer would reverberate through my life for decades. On the strength of the advance, in June I went with my parents to Utah and interviewed many of my old Mormon relatives whose stories and voices would appear in the pages of *These Latter Days*. (Gina was absolutely right; it was my second novel.) In July in the backyard of our little stucco rental house we had a never-to-be-forgotten party with international guests to celebrate Jay's having achieved his PhD in Oceanography. In August I went to Italy and returned via Mississippi (where Libby now lived) and New Orleans. Once back home in Encinitas in the fall I had a memorable dream: a large van pulled up in front of my house and all these people, strangers, piled eagerly out of it. I stood at the front door, and shouted joyfully, "You've all come here to be characters!"

It was the first of many such persistent dreams over decades, full of strangers, noisy strangers, showing up in all sorts of venues, places I do not know and have never been, clamoring to be heard, to become characters. I no longer always greet them joyfully. Some of them are cross or whiny or hungry and I wonder how I will feed them. Sometimes I try to get them to leave, chasing them out even when they are stubborn, insistent. Sometimes even asleep, I remind myself it's a dream, and trust that on waking they will dwindle, diminish, tatter, and fray with the morning light.

VI

But there were other things I wanted in addition to being an author. I wanted to have children. By the 1970s, feminists were declaring that, all in all, they, that is, we, women, did not need children to be whole human beings. The idea that children amplified one's life, like a lot of other stupid expectations, had been foisted on us by men. Children were a nuisance and if you had ambition, you couldn't be hamstrung with them. You had to be free, like men are free, to get on in life and fulfill your dreams. To want children in that era was rather like writing novels in the Structuralists' camp: to confess to it made you look silly. Ambition, achievement and babies could not be said in the same breath.

The very week I knew for certain I was pregnant with my eldest son, Tillie Olsen's *Silences* got a front page piece in the *New York Times Book Review*. *Silences* told the eloquent, heartbreaking tale of how Tillie Olsen the writer, had been submerged, even lost in the ever-present demands of her family. Tillie Olsen made Sylvia Plath and Kate Chopin sound like a chorus of minnows, especially because Tillie had not put her head in the oven; Tillie had lived to testify. Her long career—her *long delayed* career—gave depth and *gravitas* to her testimony. *Silences* suggested that for a writer to be a mother was to bind and gag your ambitions, tie yourself to the stake of obligation, light your own faggots, and burn there for the rest of your natural, unfulfilled life.

The old chills and nausea, the crippling doubt I'd felt when I read *The Bell Jar* came crawling back. More than morning sickness made me queasy as I gazed around the landscape of my life. *Beggars and Choosers*—they changed the title, but left the book intact, just as I had written it— the novel that had been the culmination of all my dreams and hopes, the book that made my heart soar out of my body when I saw it in the window of the Madison Avenue Bookshop in New York, the book whose advance I had generously donated to enhance the Italian economy, yes, that novel—did not get a front page piece in the *New York Times Book Review* like Tillie Olsen. Indeed, the *New York Times* informed my publisher they were not going to review it at all. (Although later they did. "Full of character and incident," they observed drily.) The Little, Brown editor-in-chief might have loved *Beggars*, but the sales people did not. I was informed there would be no paperback edition. Books get reviewed in hardcover, but they get widely read in paperback, so that was the end of that. Critically, *Beggars and Choosers* collected praise. Commercially it died a quiet and altogether unnoticed, unmourned death. I noticed. I mourned. For two years I could not walk into a bookstore and smell the fresh print without reliving the defeat of my dreams.

My life was about to change even more dramatically. Jay, now officially Dr. McCreary, had taken a research position in oceanography at a university lab in Fort Lauderdale,

Florida. He went there early and bought a house. I moved in the fall of 1978. Farewell to my friends, goodbye to living nearby my family, *bye-bye* to Encinitas and the small stucco house I loved. In Florida, in contrast to the growing heft and bulk of my body, I wasted away with loneliness and in a creative abyss. The independent agent who had known John Steinbeck in the 1930s retired with no replacement. I wept to get the news that my editor at Little, Brown died suddenly before he read my revision of *These Latter Days*. His replacement (or at least the editor assigned to me) had zero interest in the book. My association with Little, Brown was over. I went to work as a freelance book critic for the *Miami Herald* for fifty dollars a pop. I loved the reading (and I learned a lot) but otherwise, I was dependent, despondent, and pregnant, the marriage clearly eroding, and I loathed living in Florida.

Such friends as I met there were, naturally, Jay's associates at the lab where he went to work every day among mostly male colleagues. Their wives all had school-age children, no babies, and were primarily interested in tennis and shopping. When they found out I was a writer, they assured me they were readers. Had I read *The Bell Jar*? What a great book! At a social gathering at the lab someone referred to me as an authoress, and I responded in a less than genteel fashion. On the way driving home Jay tersely reminded me that I had a smart mouth and a sharp tongue.

"I'd rather be a bitch," I said, "than an authoress."

VII

When, a few years later when the marriage had irrevocably ended, and I lived in Redlands, California in a rented
apartment with an infant and a preschooler, when TLD had
been revised and revised once more, and yet declined again
and again, when no one wanted to read my work, when
my life unraveled, and my hopes and dreams seemed vain
and flatulent, when I thought I would die of the pain, my
mother, who had always chided me for acting as though
I lived in a book, pleaded with me: *You are a heroine! You
can and will triumph over this. Your spirit and courage and
bravado will bring you victory.*

Well, not victory, but I evaded those twin shoals of utter
despair and killing complacency. After all, I had my little
boys who were delightful, loving and fulfilling. I lived about
fifteen miles from my folks and maybe twenty miles from
my sister. My dad set up my old desk, a flat door laid across
bricks-and-boards bookshelves at either end. I plugged in
the Smith-Corona. While Bear was in pre-school and the
baby took his nap, I wrote book reviews for the *Herald*, and
the *San Jose Mercury-News*. I went to San Jose and interviewed for the job of Book Review Editor there, and didn't
get it. I returned to Redlands to face a vacuous present
and an uncertain future. I, the woman whose novel had
gleamed in the window of Madison Avenue Books in New
York City, I was scarcely a writer at all, and I sure as hell
was no heroine. When Cheerios spilled on the apartment
floor, I left them there. I fed the kids macaroni and cheese
from a box. I let them stay in their jammies all day long. I

smelled like baby spit-up because I hadn't any interest in taking a shower. Still, *These Latter Days* was finally finished, and I gathered enough unearned chutzpah, scraped up the energy to drive to the post office, and pushing Brendan in his stroller, holding Bear's hand, I stood in line, paid the postage and the SASE, and sent it out again. More rejection ensued.

And yet. Somewhere, as though far out at sea, there seemed to be a turning of the tide. My story, *Veteran's Day* written a few years before, won an international prize for short fiction, and I went to England to accept it. An editor, who rejected *These Latter Days*, did not return the manuscript to me. She asked if she could send it on to another editor, Elisabeth Scharlatt, who had left that house and gone to work for Times Books. She cautioned me Times Books (as in *New York Times*) published nothing but nonfiction, but she thought the book would appeal to Ms. Scharlatt. I wrote back and said, sure, send it on. What did I care? I certainly wasn't doing anything else with it. Six or eight months passed. Then Elisabeth Scharlatt wrote, saying how much she loved it. She acquired it in1984 and it appeared in hardcover with a beautiful jacket by Wendell Minor in 1985. *These Latter Days* was the only novel Times Books ever published.

With the advance I bought my parents a new television, I bought my sister's wedding dress. On the strength of that sale I went to New York to meet with Elisabeth Scharlatt at Times Books, and I got a new, *simpatico*, and much younger agent, Virginia Barber. I applied for and got a job (sight unseen) as Visiting Writer at a university in a Washington town on the Puget Sound. Late that summer, with my dad caravanning in the car behind us, the baby's crib strapped to the roof of his Chevy, I drove north with my two kids. We played tapes of *La Traviata* and Janis Joplin's *Pearl* all the way up there, singing along, flinging Cheerios at one another.

Settling in a new city with two little children was more difficult than I had imagined. We stayed in a motel I could ill afford, my dad looking after the kids, while I tried to find a house. I rented a place that the real estate agent told me was not a very good neighborhood. Inwardly I scoffed at him; I had grown up in the Armpit of the Nation and this place looked just fine to me. Three weeks after my dad returned to California, I had to move again; there was a neighborhood arsonist, a kid who thought it was fun to torch garages and run away, and though he hadn't torched my garage, he had struck nearby. I returned to the real estate agent and talked him into renting to me a place that was actually for sale, a shabby 1910-vintage partially furnished house where we lived for almost a year. It was so close to the university, I could walk to work. At the English department I met a young adjunct professor who helped us settle in. She also had a toddler the same age as Brendan. Moreover, she and I had shared history; she too had grown up in the Armpit of the Nation, and graduated from San Bernardino High School the same year as my brother. Fortunate chance brought me a wonderful baby-sitter, eighteen years old, who was good to and with and for my children. I found a charming co-op school for Bear situated in a farmhouse and staffed by enthusiastic teach-ers. (Public school kindergarten had a schedule that didn't suit a single parent.) After school Bear could walk to the home of a classmate whose mother kindly looked after him till I could pick him up. I rented an upright piano for ten dollars a month. I bought what we called the Tummy TV, black and white with a six-inch screen, on which we watched reruns of *The Muppet Show* on Canadian stations. My sons were happy. I was happy.

The university itself? Not so much happiness. The Eng-lish department faculty was elderly, mostly grumpy and dis-missive. They probably had no reason to be welcoming; the job was Visiting Writer for six months, and I'd be gone soon enough. (I taught there for five years.) But a few people were welcoming, and I had my own office that came with an IBM Selectric typewriter which thrilled me. I learned in a roundabout way, and to my happiness, there was a Bureau for Faculty Research who would enter my typed pages into a computer and print them for me, all for free!

But the classroom? That was the true challenge. How could I—the wayward apprentice lollygagging in front of F. Scott Fitzgerald's apartment buildings, thinking I could somehow imaginatively splash about in his leftover vibes, wishing myself into conversations with Alice B. Toklas and Gertrude Stein, and sharing aperitifs with Left Bank poets, painters and writers—stand in front of a creative writing class? I was a total fraud. I had never taken a creative writing class. I had never worked under anyone's particular guidance, or with a mentor beyond the editors who rejected my fiction with the occasional observation about the wife over-reacting. I had written fiction wholly in secret, keeping my efforts unknown to any but a very few friends. Now I was supposed to convey the elements of fiction writing to a whole classroom? I was terrified. I would surely be found out to be an imposter. (To this day I have nightmares of standing in front of a class and having nothing to say, or not being heard, myself and others recognizing my egregious inadequacy.) However, I waded into the teaching with this vow: I would never be like Gent #2 telling a writer they didn't believe in their own work, or Gent #3 swearing this story couldn't be told and reaming out anyone who tried to tell it. For template, as I walked into those classrooms, I called on my old experience teaching Freshman Comp. After all, in learning how to read well, I had learned how to write. Or maybe vice versa. To scare off the faint-of-heart I did not unroll maps across the table and marvel at them, but I assigned a shitload of reading, and set up a rigorous writing schedule. You don't like it? Leave. For anyone who stuck around, I would try to be like Gina Berriault. As teaching strategies go, these have served me and my students very well, and in that regard, I have to say, Squaw Valley was worth the pain.

Fifteen or so years after I'd first plugged in the Smith-Corona on the kitchen table, I had published two novels and had a contract for a third that was still under construction. The small, independent publisher, Graywolf, to whom I had sent *Fair Augusto and Other Stories*, kept the manuscript for two years without a word and then wrote that he loved it and wanted to publish. My literary and domestic fiction appeared here and there in literary quarterlies, and commercial magazines (including *The Lonesome Highway*, published in a journal devoted to Walt Whitman). My work had won a few prizes, and collected good reviews. But what I had really learned in those years—what I still know to be true—is this: if you are any good at all as a writer, you remain an apprentice. If you do not go on actively learning, you will atrophy artistically. Even if you go on publishing, you will atrophy. If you don't go on learning, you forget the vows implied when you picked up the pen in the first place: your task is to pursue the inspiration, and wrestle it onto the page. Revise, revisit, refine. Resist the niche. Most perilous: if you don't go on learning you will never feel that rush, the absolute, gorgeous, heart-pounding, brain-freezing thrill of breaking through a barrier you didn't even know existed until you broke it.

In continuing as a apprentice, I have made, and probably will continue to make wayward missteps, but like the Grade A Spanish critic's Grade B poet friend, I have stayed true to that standard, even that vow, even that dream.

CHAPTER SIX

REVEL AND PRESERVE

Though nothing can bring back the hour
Of splendor in the grass, of glory in the flower
We will grieve not, rather find
Strength in what remains behind.

~*William Wordsworth*
"Intimations of Immortality"
1803—1806

I

In the 1970s Encinitas, California was a sort of post-hippie-haven beach town bounded on the west by high bluffs that looked out to sea. Pacific Coast Highway, unimaginatively called First Street, served as the main street, intersecting with equally unimaginatively lettered streets going up to "K." Beyond that, at the south edge of town, the Self-Realization Fellowship serenely fronted PCH, and opened its lovely gardens to anyone who cared to come there and partake of the peace. Train whistles shrieked through, day and night, though the Encinitas depot, boarded up, sat abandoned on a strip of land allotted to the railroad. The alleys were dusty and unpaved. There was no police and we seldom even saw a sheriff's car. Moonlight Beach had lifeguards, a snack stand, fire rings and a parking lot, but if you were local, you knew where steep stairwells led down to narrow beaches with no amenities other than ropes of nasturtiums that hung down from the cliffs. When I moved to Encinitas after living five years as a transplant on the East Coast my ambition was to become a local. To achieve that, I simply had to *be*. But I had other ambitions as well. I wanted to learn to write well, and to learn to cook well. To write and cook well, I would have to actively *do*. As Julia Child says in *Mastering the Art of French Cooking*, "*Il faut mettre le main à la pâté*" ("You must put your hand to the dough") which is as fine a prescription for living as one is likely to find.

Mastering the Art of French Cooking Volume I was a birthday gift that summer. My failures and successes still stain the pages, along with scrawled notes and bookmarks. I never did master the art of French cooking, but I certainly enjoyed trying.

That I would simultaneously learn to write and learn to cook is not accidental. The learning-to-cook-well was an antidote to the pains and pangs of learning-to-write-well. They might both be performance arts in the sense that the writer needs readers (and an editor, a copyeditor, a proofer, and a publisher) but the cook only needs someone who is hungry. In cooking, everything is immediate! Ephemeral, true, but immediate! I love to feed people, and though I might spend a day in the kitchen, getting everything just right, still, in a matter of hours I can see from faces of my friends and family the pleasures I have given them. And, if I failed, well, that's immediately apparent as well. And the failure needn't be total: the soufflé that sinks in the center might still taste good, provide for the palate, even if it has disappointed the eye. And if something absolutely bombs, I early on learned to keep a dozen eggs, cheese, and some green onions on hand, and whip up a couple of omelettes and everyone laughs, and the evening can still bestow pleasure on the people who sit round the table.

Writing is just the opposite. Even if the work goes splendidly, and I could regard the day's effort with a lovely sense of having got something wonderful on the page—by the next morning that elation will have worn off. Doubt will set in. And if I got past that doubt, moved beyond the prickly stabs of Could Do Better, if eventually I was certain of the work's worth and beauty, then I took a deep breath, and sent it off to an editor (who must surely agree with me on its merit). Still, my work in that manuscript era might come back to me with mayonnaise smears or coffee stains, and a form letter that misspelled my name anyway. Now, in our electronic-era, the writer's work might rumble in the bowels of Submittable for months only to be shat out with a form letter emailed....or perhaps not ever acknowledged at all. In short—and it has ever been so since the days of

Will Shakespeare—the rewards of writing are long term. Years, even decades might elapse between the doing of the work, and the savoring of any outside rewards. Early on in my writing life, the immediate responses and rewards I got from cooking for my friends and family balanced out the long dry spells without rewards or validation from my writing.

But now that I have had decades of experience with both, I have come to believe that—putting aside the notion of reward—the writer's art and the cook's art are very much allied. Both require effort. *Il faut mettre le main à la pâté.* In doing so, you may get your hands dirty. You might have to toss out what you've wrought and begin all over again. Both require the judicious use of what's been given to you. Both rely on a process of transformation. With writing and with cooking, you take the ingredients around you, sometimes fresh-picked, sometimes long stored, you take what the soil and sunshine of your life have provided for you and you fashion from these elements something entirely else.

Henry James' famous adage: *The novelist is one on whom nothing is lost,* is absolutely true. A good cook also learns to use everything. To incorporate. As a cook or a writer you take the materials at hand and make of them, transform them into. . .what? A novel. A story. A poem. A pasta sauce. A jar of jam that reeks of summer. A peach ice cream that slides indelibly down the throat and into memory. Pesto sauce that throttles the senses with basil. In each case, in the cooking and the writing, you will have subjected these elements of your life to new processes. In creating a novel or a story or a memoir or a poem, elements and characters and bits and pieces from the author's own life are altered, put through changes, expressed, presented in a new way. Rendered into fiction or memoir there are stories fermented, stories languishing in lightless root cellars, stories still sharp with the salt of tears, stories tangy with brine, stories long since dried, and in need of heat and moisture, stories made rosy with alcohol, rueful stories rendered sugary, perhaps even over-sweet. What you want in jam is what you want as a reader—to taste not just the fruit, but the field, the sun, the very dew of the moment this fruit was picked, pulled from the vine. And in writing, as in cooking, there is sometimes no substitute for this very moment: inspiration that comes to you with the certainty of a kiss. The question is: what to do with it? Revel or preserve? This conundrum, this tension seems to me to be one of the central dilemmas certainly of my particular life. How to live, to live fully and richly and bounteously, and still be able to preserve, to process, to create, to fashion experience into Something Else.

II

This tension between revel and preserve is most clearly and classically described in the fable of the Grasshopper and the Ant which, traditionally goes like this:

An Ant was spending a frosty winter's day drying grain he had collected during the summertime. A Grasshopper, dying of hunger, passed by and earnestly begged for a little food. The Ant inquired of him, "Why did you not stock up on food during summer?" The grasshopper re-

plied, "I had no time. I passed my days singing." The Ant then said in derision, "If you are foolish enough to sing all summer, you'll dance supperless to bed in winter."

The moral here is that the Ant is justified in his refusal. The Grasshopper will, and ought to pay for his heedless reveling. The Ant will be rewarded for his steadfast preservation. And perhaps for most of human history, this might well have been true. It's almost impossible now for us to re-create, even to imagine just how nasty brutish and short (to quote Thomas Hobbes) life actually was for centuries. People endured the cruel, cold dark winters lit only by candles, warmed only by fuel that needed to be cut and kept dry; they cooked on open hearths, and drank unclean water. In centuries long past, the contrast of summer with winter must have been so fabulously dramatic that it's no wonder the Church filled these days with religious meaning, saints' days or festivals that come at (more or less) six week intervals throughout the year. In the long distant past think of those last weeks of winter so grim, Lenten fasting of necessity. In contrast, the advent of spring must truly have felt like resurrection. The coming of fall, the end of summer so filled with portent. The harvest kept people alive through the winter; the lack of a harvest brought famine. They went to bed, their guts cramping from hunger, and woke the same way.

The preservation of food was essential to the preservation of life itself. People kept root crops in the ground or under straw. They preserved vegetables in oil. They preserved fish and meat in salt. They preserved eggs and herbs in acidic vinegars. When they could, they preserved fruit in alcohol. They preserved apples and chestnuts by drying. They preserved cabbage and cucumbers by fermentation. They preserved summer fruits in jam thick with sugar. The phrase "to put up," rings often in old cookbooks, meaning to preserve against the inroads of time, which is to say, against rot. To revel in the present, that is, to fail to "put up," invites future rot.

Historically, mortals probably took little delight from their cooking. Most of humanity took only sustenance from what they ate, asking no more than that it should give them the strength needed to go on, day to day. When I was researching what to feed my nineteenth century Parisian working class characters in *Cosette*, I was struck by the paucity, the awful tedium of their diet, bread, apples, perhaps a thin gruel or soup. And this is the diet of the French, renowned for their culinary traditions?

John Burnet the social historian of English working class life conjectures in his compelling *Plenty and Want* that though coffee and tea were both popular in England by the end of the eighteenth century, tea became the national drink because of the demands of the Industrial Revolution when people's lives—their very sense of time—irrevocably changed. Their days no longer reflected the diurnal progress of the sun; time came to be carved up, not so much by the tolling of the church bells, but by the shriek of factory whistles. Time became finite increments of labor. Even though sociability evolved in these situations, meals were basically time to re-fuel the workers. Workers drank tea because tea can be steeped. Coffee must be brewed. To these observations, Sidney Mintz in his social history of cane sugar, *Sweetness and Power*, offers the observation that for workers, a cup of hot sweetened tea transformed a cold meal into a hot meal. And sugar not only sweetened the tea, but provided energy that the body needed in terms of what we would now call empty calories. They were not empty then. As my father used to say, quoting from his impoverished, rural, Depression-era childhood, "What won't fatten will fill."

When I visited my dad's Aunt Lila she was in her seventies, a fine cook and vocal proponent of "putting things up," which is a long-standing Mormon tradition. With what she had "put up" she fed everyone with an unstudied charm and generosity that came from deep within her spirit and her Mormon convictions. Aunt Lila reveled in what she had preserved—and so did everyone else, Saint or sinner, who came within her orbit. As people showed up at her house she just kept opening up jars of fruit, pickles, onions, beans, beets, all of which gleamed in jars on her shelves.

In the novel *These Latter Days*, and in fictions that evolved from it, I have loosely cast Aunt Lila as one of my favorite characters, Afton Lance. Afton has an older brother, the studious and devout Gideon Douglass who toils on his Great Timetable. In the novel Gideon is yoked in an unhappy marriage to the irreverent and unsuitable Kitty, originally a Mormon convert from England. In the summer of 1918 from his study window, Gideon glances out into the backyard, to the peach tree in the backyard to see

Tootsie, four years old, playing in the grass where Kitty lies, barefoot and shirtless, her blouse hanging from a branch like a flag of truce, her skin tinting pink, her arm outflung.

The half naked Tootsie sat beside her, splattered with peach meat and bees around his head. They must have thought him an enormous ambulating flower. Around them both, fallen fruit rotted into the earth and the flies droned. Kitty waved them away as she bit into a peach, and the juices ran down her mouth into her hair. She flung to the earth what she did not want, and went on singing a tune from her music hall days. Gideon's first thought was to yank his son and his half-clad wife inside, to impress upon her respectability and decorum, to suggest that peaches should not be squandered, but properly put up in Mason jars, that this was the duty of a wife. But he didn't. And he knew he would never again suggest to Kitty that she preserve from one summer to the next what was clearly to be relished in a single golden moment.

Kitty, like the Grasshopper, is all for sensory immediacy; she cares nothing for long-term savor. Gideon, the Ant, is committed to preservation. My personal loyalties are ambivalent. I have vast affection for Kitty who is shallow, vain, impudent, lacking any sort of moral fiber. But my work in life has ended up being much more like the bookish Gideon's task: a reader, a teacher, a writer, a person engaged in preservation. Serious teachers and serious writers, that's what we do: preserve what we have learned, season it, and send it out to someone else.

But isn't that too what the good cook does? Savor the summer season and make raspberry jam from those few weeks when they are at their peak. Or the pesto sauce I make and freeze when the basil is at its best, its height of flavor. One winter evening when I put this pesto on spaghetti, my youngest son remarked, "It's not like a sauce, it's like an emotion."

As a fiction writer I aspire to that same high compliment from the reader: that what is before that reader is not mere words on paper, but an emotion. In every book or story, or memoir I preserve certain moments: golden moments or leaden moments, moments redolent of rosemary for remembrance, friendship and love, or tainted with the bitter herb rue for remorse or fear. I aspire to preserve these moments in the old brine of language, in sweet and sour prose. Professionally and personally I struggle with the question: is it possible to have both sensory-immediate satisfaction and long-term savor?

III

My last address in Encinitas was a small rental house on H Street, built in the 1920s, a block from the bluffs overlooking the ocean and two blocks from PCH. At this time my sister, Helen, a teacher, lived up in the hills above Palm Springs. Helen had rented a house that had half a dozen plum trees, the undistinguished, perfectly ordinary prune-plum variety. These trees looked innocent in the fall when she'd moved in, but by July they had gone berserko. My sister was knee-deep in prune-plums. She couldn't give them away and she couldn't eat them and they were splatting all over the ground, driving the flies and bees and the raccoons mad with joy. Perhaps responding to some old Mormon impulse deep in her DNA Helen called me up, and said on Saturday she was bringing these plums down to my house and we were going to "put them up." I protested that we didn't have any idea how to put them up, and she said, well, we'll learn then. She told me to go to the store and buy a bunch of jars and lids. No doubt the jars and lids would have directions for how to "put things up."

Helen drove the hundred-some-odd miles with boxes of plums, with a few fugitive, stowaway flies and bees, all of them probably drunk with pleasure as these plums going off by the minute, getting riper, rotting by the mile. At last she came to my house by the beach, and together we hauled these boxes of dusty plums into the small kitchen where I had set up the vats of boiling water. We went to work following the instructions that came with the jars and lids. I think Aunt Lila would have been proud of us, though no doubt she would have been critical as well.

We were at it all afternoon and into the evening, and by the end we were purple to the elbows and our clothes were streaked with purple and we had purple under our fingernails and purple all over the sink, and plums had fallen splat, like purple Rorschach tests on the floor. The bees and flies at the bottom of the box, unwitting travelers, staggered around the house and flung themselves drunkenly against the windows. We were a mess, but when we were through we had them all lined up, jars and jars of these formerly undistinguished plums that had been somehow transformed into a thing of beauty. They were the most lovely color I had ever beheld. What was gleaming in those jars bore almost no relation to the dusty, dirty, rotting plums Helen had hauled down the mountain, as though from all of that raw fruit, we had beauty incarnate in these jars. So beautiful that I kept my last jar on the bookcase just to look at its dazzling color. I gave the rest away as gifts.

If what I am writing here, now, were a story or a novel, or a poem, I might close with the observation that I still had these brilliant plums in their jar, and how they still inspire me. Or I might say on some portentous day or another, the jar dropped and broke and the plums and their inky beauty spilled, metaphorically informing me that whole part of my life was sadly over. I might endow them with dramatic significance, because in a novel or a poem significance reverberates just under or hovers just over everything. A memoir however aspires to truth, whether or not it has any particular significance. Truthfully, none of these meaningful things happened. Somewhere in the flux and flow of many moves between 1978 and 1984, that jar of purple plums just vanished. I don't remember how or when. The plums, preserved against time, vanished into time. Gone.

And yet, they remain for me so vivid in memory! Helen and I created ephemeral, purple works of art; we transformed what was rotting into a thing of beauty, if not a joy forever. That afternoon seemed to me one of the few in which revel and preserve were balanced, simultaneous, as though the Ant and the Grasshopper had struck their truce at last, and went off arm in arm.

CHAPTER SEVEN

"INCHBESSESS"

You are as many a person as the languages you know
~Armenian Proverb

Not promising, I thought to myself. Not what you think of when you move to Hawaii, three stories of ugly apartments set atop garages near the top of a hill. Staring up at the Faculty Family Housing complex at the University of Hawaii Manoa, the place looked to me to be a sort of concrete slum, a housing project. My husband, my little son and I got out of the rented car and, hauling our suitcases and backpacks, we made our way from the parking lot up the concrete open-air stairwell that was dirty with debris and childish scrawl passing for graffiti. At the top of the three-story stairwell, we looked down a long, concrete walkway fronted, on the left, by apartments, on the right by metal railings. As we walked past these open doors and windows many sounds tumbled out, televisions, radios, cries of babies, people chattering in languages unknown to me. Clearly many of these families had been camped here for years. People hung their laundry over the railings, and grew pots of wan herbs by their doors. Little children played along the walkway, and scents of wonderfully exotic cooking wafted as we passed each door, enough to make you want to linger just to inhale. Our apartment was about midway down this long line. Jay put the key in the lock, and we stepped in; the interior was every bit as soul-killing ugly as the exterior. But wait! I dropped the suitcase, and crossed to the sliding glass door, opened it, and walked out onto the balcony. Look at that! Diamond Head and the distant Pacific! A swath of sky and sea and city! Honolulu spread out before us! A million-dollar view from Faculty Family Housing! I pulled out a kitchen drawer, brought it to the balcony, and turned it over so two-year-old Bear could stand on it, and see the dazzling view we would have for the whole summer of 1981.

Family Faculty Housing might have looked like a grim project, but the place was an extraordinary living experience. Our neighbors were all interesting, international people from different cultures and countries and disciplines, some of which I had never heard of (Gerontology?). They were mostly young families like ours, and the place was crawling with kids. With some other Faculty Housing kids Bear attended Manoa Montessori School in a serene Buddhist garden. He made lots of friends, Jay and I made lots of friends, and we went to many parties and beach picnics. My mom and sister visited. That summer of 1981 passed, muddled in retrospect, into a general sense of communal well-being. One incident, however, is singularly seared into memory.

Jay and our longtime friend, Joel Picaut from France had joined another scientist friend, Dennis Moore, for the summer at UH working on El Niño. One afternoon in August Jay called home, and behind his voice I could hear all kinds of laughter and roistering. He said the Soviet Union's oceanographic research vessel had come into the Port of Honolulu and Soviet scientists had invited University of Hawaii oceanographers to come aboard. Remember, in 1981 the Soviets were still fighting the Afghans; indeed, America had refused to participate in the 1980 Olympics that were held in the Soviet Union to punish them for invading Afghanistan. In short the Cold War was in fine fettle and so the invitation to come aboard the Soviets' ship was an unusual one. In fact it was rare in those days for a Soviet research vessel to be allowed into the port of Honolulu at all.

Jay said that he and Joel and Dennis and the other UH oceanographers had been on board all afternoon, drinking vodka and talking science. Science was waning, but the party was just warming up. Why didn't I get a baby-sitter for Bear and come down to the harbor?

"How will I know which is the Soviet vessel?" I asked.

"Oh, you'll know it. It's berthed next to the *Kana-Keoki*, the University of Hawaii's research ship."

Indeed no one could have mistaken the proud Queen Mary of a Soviet research vessel parked next to the *Kana-Keoki*. Poor, diminished and plug-ugly, the *Kana-Keoki* sat in the shadow of the gorgeous, gleaming Soviet vessel. The plank was down, and a friend and I wandered on board, greeted with smiles, which we understood and language we didn't. We found Jay, Joel, Dennis, and the men from the UH lab who, by this time, had altogether forsaken science for laughter and music and drinking. Jay introduced us to Sergei who spoke fluent English, the only one who spoke English at all. Sergei served as translator for everyone.

These Soviet scientists were generous and courteous, in fact downright courtly. They showed us around the ship and shared pictures of their families and gave away cigarettes and candy and gewgaws, pins and mementoes of the 1980 Moscow Olympics, something few Americans would have, indeed, few would have seen.

Everyone eventually gathered in the spacious galley and dining room bedecked with the hammer and sickle Soviet flags. Jay and the others were drinking vodka with the captain, some officers and scientists. One of them started to laugh, clearly and pointedly at Jay. Jay asked Sergei "Why is he laughing at me?"

At first Sergei declined to say why, but finally he said, "It's because you drink like a woman."

Jay was sipping his vodka, not chugging it. Noting that their vodka bottles were half the size of a fifth, Jay replied, "That's only because your Russian vodka bottles are so small!" A reply that made everyone laugh.

The galley was outfitted with a small stage and a microphone and one by one the Soviet crew and scientists played different instruments, sang solos and duets; they put Russian music on the stereo, and danced those incredibly athletic dances, their arms crossed, their feet kicking out from the knees. As each of the performers came on, Sergei told us a bit about their various backgrounds, what they did on the ship and so on.

Then there came up to sing a swarthy man; he had a full beard, dark eyes, thick brows and a high nose; he was probably my age, early thirties. He stood and sang the saddest song I have ever heard. Everyone who had been cheering, clapping time for the other singers, dancers and musicians quieted. Sergei whispered to me that the man was singing about the sadness of his people, the losses, the heartbreaking separations. Sergei said he was a surgeon, fulfilling a state service requirement on this vessel. He was an Armenian.

"Really?" I said, "I am Armenian." And I told him my name, not the name I was born with or married to, but the name I had chosen, Laura Kalpakian.

When this man finished singing, Sergei beckoned him to our table and introduced us. Then he said that I was an Armenian. The surgeon's face lit. Never in my life has a stranger looked at me with such affection, with such warmth, and such happiness! From all those Armenian church picnics I had attended with my grandmother where smoke from the kebab fires swirled amid the dust, the heat, the gnarled geraniums, the old women pinching my cheek and pulling me into a hug against the buttons on their dresses, from all that memory I drew the one word my grandmother had taught me for these occasions. *Inchbessess*. Basically, hello.

The surgeon took me into his embrace and called me his sister! This man sailing under the hammer and sickle of the Soviet Union embraced me, my husband, my friends. From that moment linguistic barriers, if they did not crumble, at least they cracked; these fissures were helped along by more drinking and feelings of such warmth and camaraderie. With Sergei's help we talked and exchanged info and pictures of children and families. The surgeon showed the picture of his beautiful wife in Armenia; he was the father of two sons, near in age to our Bear. The Armenian surgeon (whose name, sadly, I have forgotten) insisted he should cook Armenian dinner for me, my husband, for the other American scientists who had gathered around to watch what looked like a family reunion, never mind this Armenian man and I were strangers, and did not share a language. Perhaps if I knew how to speak Armenian, all this would have been easier, but I did not. Never mind, tomorrow night, we all somehow agreed, tomorrow the Soviet scientists would come to faculty housing. The surgeon would bring an Armenian dish. We would all contribute something. The party was to be in Joel's ground floor apartment in faculty housing for unmarried people.

On Saturday Jay and Dennis and Joel spent all afternoon borrowing chairs and tables and lining them up at Joel's. We Americans, the scientists, the wives and girlfriends (yes, the scientists were all men) all brought salads and desserts and cold beer. We were about twelve in number. Sergei, the Armenian surgeon and a third Soviet scientist, Eugene, arrived at Faculty Housing before dusk. How these

Soviets got permission to get off the ship and come to the University of Hawaii, I do not know. By what means of transportation they came from their ship, I do not know. I only know they showed up. They brought vodka, wine, musical instruments. The Armenian surgeon brought the main dish, *derev*, enough for all of us, and we kept it warm in Joel's oven. He had spent the entire afternoon cooking.

That night the parents in faculty housing had all been apprised of a must-attend theatrical event that would be staged on a low hillside that sloped down to the parking lot. The play, "Cinderella," had been organized, that is, directed and produced by a particularly bossy little girl, age ten, who had rounded up every kid who was out of diapers, and gave them roles. (Bear was a page or a herald to the prince.) She, naturally, starred. Our Soviet guests joined us and the other parents in the parking lot. The young international cast collected much applause from everyone, including the Soviets who didn't need English to be enchanted by the production. Children too can provide a universal language.

After the play we wended our way to Joel's apartment. Night had fallen, and the jalousied windows were open and the palm trees rustling in the trade winds, and the thick scent of plumeria wafted in. We laid out all the food, which itself constituted a sort of language of taste and delight. Eugene and the Armenian surgeon could speak some French, and I had schoolgirl French, and when necessary, Joel could translate for us. We let music and laughter express our feelings, even if we could not well express our thoughts. We ate and drank, and in the course of this long meal each of the Soviet scientists pushed back his chair, rose, raised his glass, more than once, and offered toasts. Sergei translated. The Americans too stood and offered toasts and Sergei translated for us as well. For all our mirth as we raised our glasses and our voices, one by one, the occasion took on a sort of solemnity, a sort of diplomatic mission of the heart.

We saluted peace between our countries. Peace in the world. We drank to the hope that the camaraderie, the affection and respect created here, this night, in Honolulu, in the middle of the Pacific, would be a harbinger for the future, for the hope that our children could one day meet in peace as friends and comrades, that political boundaries would fall and understanding ensue. We were, all of us, Americans and Soviets, brought up on opposite sides of the Cold War, and these toasts were so moving, we got misty.

In 1981 none of us, Americans or Soviets, could have foretold that in a decade these men would not be Soviet citizens. They would once again be Russians or Armenians, Ukrainians, whatever else their ancestors had been born to. In 1981 no one at that table could have foreseen that the fall of the Soviet Union in 1989 would stand in history, a landmark, like 1789, the end of an era.

After the meal, after the solemn toasts, the scientists broke out their instruments and performed again, the Armenian surgeon singing a new song, not so sad. The Americans too, I think performed, but the particulars escape me, due to all the vodka and the wine, though I do remember that communication was suddenly easier, especially when we put American rock and roll on the stereo, turned up the volume, and the dancing began. No language barrier there.

At a certain point Eugene decided they must leave. Like Cinderella hearing the stroke of midnight, the other two immediately jumped up and obeyed. After the Russians left, the cops came because neighbors had complained about the noise. The cops asked to see ID from Joel. They issued grave warnings about the noise. They broke up the party and left. After they'd gone, we all agreed: good thing the Soviets weren't here. The cops might have felt differently about the noise if the party included Soviet citizens. But, worse, imagine what *The Soviets* would have thought of the black uniforms, the white helmets, the nightsticks and firearms, the no-nonsense warnings that the neighbors had turned us in.

A few years later at a scientific meeting in England, Jay again saw Sergei and Eugene. They remembered him, and that night in Honolulu. They spoke of it fondly. Jay always believed that one or both men acted as KGB agents, and I have to agree. No doubt that's how permission to leave the Soviet research vessel was granted at all. After the fall of the Soviet Union, Jay never again saw them at international meetings, and word was that the gleaming, gorgeous Soviet research vessel had been sold off.

Where is that Armenian surgeon now? The man who on the strength of my single Armenian word, *Inchbessess*, embraced me and mine, where is he? Where is his wife whose picture he so proudly showed? Where are the sons he so hoped would meet my son? I wonder if in the course of the all-too-human events which have befallen Russia and Armenia, the world, for that matter, does he ever think back to August 1981 when a single Armenian word united us all? Does he remember the trade winds blowing through the open windows, the glasses raised in toasts to peace, humanity, and brotherhood?

Though his name has eluded my memory, I shall never forget him, or that evening in Honolulu when I experienced the power of the diaspora: that a single Armenian word could connect an American woman with a person from the Soviet Union, could unite us in a shared tradition, though we did not speak the same language, and though our lives were incomparably different. That August evening makes me believe that all those whom history has persecuted, denied reviled and finally exiled—the Jews, the Chinese, the Irish, the Indians, the Armenians, the Vietnamese, the Syrians, any culture or country whose people have been pushed out, away, into a diaspora—are endowed, of necessity, with a complex identity, with a complex empathy, able, with one word, to strike connection, affection, respect, regard among strangers.

CHAPTER EIGHT

OF BOOKS AND BOYS

The Child is father of the Man.
~William Wordsworth
"My Heart Leaps Up When I Behold"
1802

I returned to his room, and stood there, desolate in the doorway. He had taken a couple of suitcases and a trunk to USC. He had left a lot of chaos. Mateless socks peered from under the bed; T-shirts and towels lay rumpled together. The clock radio blinked away—12:00 AM! 12:00 AM!—cheerfully oblivious that Bear had gone. I waded into the archeological dig where the remains of my eldest son's childhood lay uncovered.

I noticed for the first time in years Bear's eighth-grade painting hanging by itself on the tack-studded wall. All the other posters were rolled, packed and on their way to the university, as was the stereo, the computer, the microphone cords and music. Except for the dictionary, thesaurus, and Bartlett's *Book of Quotations*, the books remained behind.

261

My eldest had only just left home, but his room seemed long-deserted, and the great vacancy heartbreaking.

Adrift in this rubble I was struck with a curious feeling of déjà vu, no doubt because bringing up children is very like writing books. Like books, children absorb you, heart and soul, for a certain number of years. And even when they are finished, and need to leave home, I fear they are not ready for the world. I lose sleep, I suffer, not so much over what I have done, but what I have left undone.

With every book I've written, the manuscript has had to be coaxed from my hands, the editor's deadline past due, everyone insistent that I must part with the manuscript *now*. When I do, finally, send it off, there's a sense of relief, but once I return to my study where it was drafted, I am desolate. Research materials lie about like discarded clothing. Dog-eared half-drafts loll off the shelves. Quotes and notes and pictures are still pinned to the wall. But the novel hath fled and the private, finite world of writing hath ended. The emptiness overwhelms me. The silence is deafening.

When Bear was a toddler and we lived in Florida, I took to writing with a pen because the *tap tap tap* of the typewriter alerted him instantly that I was working. He recognized that the typewriter was his only serious competition for my undivided attention. When he heard the keys rattling, he would waddle in and pull all the books off the lower shelves, and look at me with a confident grin: *Even if I'm in trouble, I don't care. You know I'm cute. You know you can't resist me.* So in order to work without his interruption (it's true, I could not resist him) two days a week, I'd unplug the typewriter and take it to a deserted trailer on the property of Jay's lab where they'd given me space to work.

Each day, as I drove out of the driveway, Bear would stand on the porch bawling out my name in a great peal of pain.

"Mama!"

The sound of his voice, the sight of his sturdy little self, tears streaming down his face, broke my heart. Arriving at work, I'd immediately phone home to Mary Tocci, our neighbor, and an Italian grandmother who stayed with Bear. I'd ask anxiously if he was okay. Mary (who had raised six children of her own) assured me Bear was just fine. The melodrama was for my benefit alone. As soon as my car was out of sight, Mary said, he dried his tears, and got on with his own very important day.

Now Bear was eighteen years, instead of eighteen months, and I was enduring this experience in reverse. As I moved aimlessly about his deserted room, I chided myself for not drying my eyes and getting on with my own important day. I reminded myself sternly that his leaving was imperative, necessary for us both. Besides, we were not irrevocably parted. Bear would come home again.

Bear would come home. But my boy? That was the loss, wasn't it? Bear is no longer my boy. He would not be my boy, a child again. He would always be my son. My son had gone to university far away.

When I went to a university far away, my mother, though reluctant to see me go, helped me pack. I am chagrined to admit now I cannot even remember her tears. My own eagerness for adventure, however, remains vivid: The Girl of the Golden West was about to see something of the east coast! The great world! That was how I thought of it at the time. I scarcely noticed my mother's brave ambivalence. She folded things neatly in my suitcase. She had packed my mental trunk as well. But less neatly. This mental trunk bulged with advice and admonitions, values and vagaries, morsels culled from Bartlett's Book of Parental Quotations.

And what became of that mental trunk once I'd left? Figuratively speaking, I kicked it downstairs. I smiled, delighted as it crashed and smashed and splintered. I left it there, spilled, open in the metaphorical distant dark, while I plunged into new adventures, heedless of my mother's advice and careless of her feelings. So confident was I in my freedom from childhood's grasp, I had not even brought with me a picture of my mother and father.

Then one day someone asked me what did my mother look like? I was embarrassed and perplexed, and except to note that she had dark hair and eyes (as do I) I was unequal to the task. I could see my mother's face, of course. I could hear her voice, read her words in the annotated copy of Bartlett's Parental Quotations (where I could be found under *Daughters, errant*), but I could not describe her. I called home and asked for a picture.

When Bear left for college, I made certain he had pictures of me. I gave him copies of my books, though I knew he would not read them. And yet, as we were getting ready for him to leave, I would wake in the night with a vague sense of panic, the same sort that often torments me in the latter stages of writing a book: What crucial element have I neglected? What have I not sufficiently stressed?

Books can undergo many revisions, but with Bear, I knew these questions were as pointless as they were painful. I had had eighteen years to impress upon him my values. Whatever I had left undone or unsaid, it could not be done now. It could not be said now. But as his departure drew nearer, I tried nonetheless. I repeated myself endlessly. I packed Bear's mental trunk—as I packed his suitcases—with everything I could think of. No one in our family travels light.

Buckle up. Recycle. Trust your instincts. Take care of your health. Pick up your clothes. Phone home. Take your vitamins. Never show up as a guest empty-handed. Expand your notions of relevance, and your world will expand correspondingly. Find time to dream. Find joy in your work. Speak a foreign language. Learn to cook. Live up to your responsibilities. Don't fear emotion. Good manners will serve you always. Good friends, good food, good music, good books will reward you always. Floss. Fall in love.

As adults, we look at childhood with dual perspectives: as parents, and as sons and daughters. As parents we know that on leaving home, sons and daughters kick that mental trunk downstairs and listen with some delight as it crashes, smashes and breaks open. We also know that we spend thirty years picking through the wreckage at the foot of the stairs. We hunch in the darkness as we sift and separate, weighing the worth of what we've been taught. Tumbled from those mental trunks, still bright, even in the murk of years, are the shards of wisdom, those transcendent bits we recognize and pass on to our children.

I had parted with my eldest son, as with a book I'd worked on for eighteen years. When I returned to his room, I surveyed the rumpled remains of our long togetherness, our mutual, private past, of Bear's childhood, finite and private and finished. He was happy. I was happy for him, but I was sad as well.

In a desultory, uninspired fashion, I began picking up the litter of leaving: laundry basket for the socks and towels, recycle bags for the paper and pop cans. The emptiness was everywhere eloquent, the silence painful. I wanted to go stand on the porch and wail, "Bear!" in a great peal of pain. But instead, I called my mother.

CHAPTER NINE

ANOTHER STORY

To be alive at all is to have scars.

~*John Steinbeck*

The Winter of Our Discontent

1961

T his is not my story. I wasn't even there. But like a stone well-worn, polished by the waters that run over it, this story has come to have a pleasing roundness in our family, the sharp edges, the pain buffed away. It is my mother's story, how she became a convert to John Steinbeck. She tells it well, as someone might recount discovering the True Faith. Like most converts, she is emphatic, vocal, eager to spread Steinbeck's Word. Her conversion story testifies to expanding one's notions of what is relevant. Do not be narrow-minded: that's the implicit moral in the pain-free version. Like most such time-honed tales, the story itself can be reduced to a sort of punchline. The poignancy is in the context, always left unspoken in the telling.

In 1969 my sister's high school home tutor required her to read *Cannery Row*. Helen loved it and she urged my mother to read it. But my mother said, *Oh no, I don't like Steinbeck*. My sister asked what she had read that she didn't like. And to this my mother rather shame-facedly replied, *Nothing*. She had never read a book by Steinbeck.

Why had she not read him? As a girl growing up in Los Angeles in the 1930s Peggy Kalpakian had absorbed urban prejudices against the Okies pouring into California. Steinbeck of course was associated with them, and with other generally unsavory Not Nice people. But my mother agreed with Helen that this was an ancient prejudice and so she read *Cannery Row*. Read *Tortilla Flat*. Read *Sweet Thursday*. The punchline to this story? After she started reading Steinbeck's novels, my mom became an avid fan! But there is a story beyond the punchline.

My mother moved from the charms of *Cannery Row* to *The Grapes of Wrath*, and *Mice and Men*, *In Dubious Battle*, on to the tapestry of Shakespearean struggle in *East of Eden*. As she waded further and deeper into Steinbeck's work and life, she quit getting the books from the library. She bought them all. Bought multiple copies. Pressed these books into the hands of unbelievers, or even the merely indifferent, saying, *Steinbeck is a wonderful writer. Here is a book you will love. Read*. But her conversion was not an altogether literary experience. John Steinbeck rescued my mother, as surely as if he placed his hand at her elbow and walked her through a dark time.

When she became a True Believer, I did not live there. I was three thousand miles from Southern California, living back East going to graduate school and contributing my feet, my voice to the protest, to antiwar marches.

When I was back East, my brother Doug was six thousand miles west of California. Vietnam. Serving in the US Army, Fourth Infantry. His letters home from Vietnam were erratic, erratically received and erratically written. Reading his letters, which were terrible, terrifying and enigmatic, my parents feared. They despaired when there was silence. Strange phone calls came to my parents' house, cryptic inquiries, references to military prison from the parents of a boy in his unit. (And they were boys, make no mistake; my brother was in the Fourth Infantry, thrashing through Vietnamese jungles at nineteen because he had wantonly dropped a course at the community college, no longer a full-time student, and thus, ripe for the draft.)

My parents woke each morning sick with unspeakable foreboding and went to bed each night sick with unspoken grief. During the day, in addition to their ordinary jobs—a secretary, a pharmaceutical rep—they bore these unshared, unbearable burdens. How can you tell the neighbors, the supercilious boss, the client whose business you need, that you fear for your son's life, his health, his freedom, his sanity? In these same years, my parents trembled too at the prospect of losing my sister. At seventeen, stalked by Crohn's disease, Helen was too frail to go to school. She underwent one massive surgery after another, none proving successful.

Into this daily vat of anxiety and dread, unexplained illness, the possibility of death in a distant jungle, there came into my mother's life the austere presence of John Steinbeck. Steinbeck's books, his vision, his characters, his prose spoke to her. Steinbeck stood beside my mother in the way that old gods might have stood beside sufferers, save that my family's old gods had dissipated. The Mormon faith that had sustained my father's people was not my mother's faith (nor by that time, my father's either). The Armenian Apostolic church that had sustained her parents relied on a language she did not understand. The protestant faith of her youth seemed smug, unquestioning, unequal to the incipient tragedy that gnawed at her sleep and greeted her on waking. But Steinbeck was equal to the possibility of tragedy. Steinbeck recognized sorrow when he met it. He knew struggle. Steinbeck's rolling prose became a kind of Holy Writ. My mother cut passages out of his books and pasted them inside of the cupboard door where she kept her good china, where, she could secretly open it anytime and read when she needed sustenance.

Steinbeck's characters do not (to paraphrase Faulkner) prevail. But they endure. And there are times when the enduring is sufficient. Indeed, when it is all that's possible, when the enduring itself bestows on suffering a kind of invisible nobility, which, in turn, creates courage. My mother—her life outwardly ordinary, middle class—found herself like Steinbeck's Okies, and like his beleaguered workers, like the limited Lennie, like farmers facing drought. She was overwhelmed by forces she did not understand and could not control. These characters gave her the courage to endure. Beyond his books, Steinbeck's own life and personal struggles, his hard work, his self-doubt, all that spoke to her. When she read that his son had been in Vietnam, my mother knew that he understood. In some strange way, John Steinbeck stood at her side. A grizzled ghost.

That he too was a Californian helped. Steinbeck's pastures of heaven were hers. He wrote of things and people, the light, the fields, the landscape, sensory experience my mother could easily picture, remember. His prose was not Shakespearean, shaped in memorable but arcane constructions; his sentences were hewn in California, beside the Pacific, in and of the long valleys. In the winters of her discontent, dread and anxiety, Steinbeck, his characters, his words, his evocations, his tragic vision came to my mother's rescue when she most needed rescue, when all else failed.

My brother needed rescuing. One at a time she mailed Steinbeck's novels to Doug. Those books may still be in Vietnam.

Young and full of my own endeavors, I did not need to be rescued, but she sent me the novels too. I read them. I was a literary enthusiast, but not altogether a convert. Steinbeck's work whispered to me that fiction could be created from the dust, the dry wind, the tumbleweed and oleander, from anonymous arroyos, the canyons of the California that I knew.

My sister endured, survived; indeed, she prevailed, and had a long, fulfilling career as a Special Ed teacher, and a respected member of California Horseman's Association/ Equestrian Trails Patrol.

My brother came home from Vietnam. But that is another story.

ACKNOWLEDGMENTS

To write a memoir is to take the sand, the particular grains of sand, and shape them into a sandcastle. Let me acknowledge individually these particular people.

As is clear in these pages I owe a lifelong debt of gratitude to my mother, Peggy Kalpakian Johnson, to my late father, Bill Johnson, to my sweet, generous sister, Helen Johnson. Ongoing thanks to my talented daughter-in-law, Raya Yarbrough, to my wonderful sons, Bear and Brendan McCreary, to their dad, Jay McCreary, and to my lovely granddaughters, Sonatine Yarbrough McCreary and Zai Pakradouhi McCreary.

For their insight, translations, and many contributions to the family, I thank my cousins, Patty and Jenk Stephenson. For their insight, translations, their willingness to revisit the past, I thank my distant cousins, Astrid Kaloustian and her mother, Arminee Kaloustian, and my distant cousins, Nina and Haig Krakirian, Thanks too to novelist Nancy Kricorian for her time-saving guidance.

Immeasurable gratitude to Connie Feutz, who offered valuable early insight on all these essays in their still-struggling-and-straggling drafts. And thanks to the writers who brought their editorial thoughts and suggestions: Andrea Gabriel, Janna Jacobson, Frances Howard-Snyder, Victoria Doerper, Brenda Wilbee, Carol McMillan, Laura Rink, Cami

Ostman, Pam Helberg and Virginia Herrick. To Joe Nolting, Nancy Taylor, Roy Taylor, Linda Morrow, and Jes Stone I owe gratitude for support and community.

I remain indebted to my longtime literary agents, Juliet Burton and Pamela Malpas for their steadfast enthusiasm. I also remember with gratitude the late Gina Berriault, Virginia Barber, Kit Ward, Ned Bradford, Meredith Cary and R. D. Brown.

Acknowledgments are like sundials; they only count the sunny hours. So *merci mille fois* to those who appear happily, even if nameless in these pages: Bill Robertson and Gail Meadows, Connie and Bob Eggers, Judy Langen and Bill Langen, Linda and Larry Cox, Susie and Lance Woeltjen, Joan and Ed Lovitt, Libby Nybakken and Bill Graves, Judith Brown, Patty Bruland, Kim Carney, Liz Eck, Kathy Frank, Terry Harrington, June Howard, Judy Hunt, Elaine Lui, Vincent Loris, Bill Mazzacane, Frankie McHenry, Debra Mipos, Dennis Moore, Ilene Nelson, Tom Molyneaux, Margaret Ann Marchioli, Mary Marchioli, Mary Tocci, Joel Picaut, Mary Sullivan, Paola Rizzoli, Bob Schmorleitz.

To the Founder, CEO—in fact, the Inspiration, the Rock-and-a-Shelter—of Paint Creek Press, Andrea Gabriel, abundant ongoing thanks and applause for her many skills, her understanding of my shortcomings, and her high-spirited undertaking of this fine, fun venture in the first place

ADANA, TURKEY

KALPAKIANS

Hagop 1853—1931 and Meribe Kalpakian (b. c.1860 d.c
1930 in Romania)
Five children:
    Mannik (or Mannig) 1884—1950
    Haroutune 1887—1963 Became Harry Kalpakian [author's grandfather]
      m. Haigouhi (Helen) Koulahksouzian, four daughters
    Garabed (1890—1959) m. one daughter
    Zabelle (1896—1970) d. in Damascus, Syria
      m. Khatchadour Krakirian in 1915.
      Four children
    Nishan 1902—1970 d. in France m. Nevart Hekimian
    1911—1981 two children

KOULAHKSOUZIANS

Asdoor and Ysabet, parents, both died 1915 or 1916
Four children:
    Asdoor Koulahksouzian 1884—1940 [Became Art
    Clark]
      married twice, no children

275

Dudu Koulahksouzian Boyd 1887—1939
  m. Hovanness Boyajian who became John Boyd, two
  children
Haigouhi Koulahksouzian Kalpakian (Helen) 1901—
1987 [author's grandmother]
  m. Haroutune Kalpakian (became Harry Kalpakian)
  five children
Haigauz Koulahksouzian 1905–1987 became Harry
Clark
  m. Martha Hallalian, no children

Miss Grace Towner 1883—1968
  Born in Delphos, Kansas, died in Claremont, California,
  spent her career in Turkey as a missionary. Principal of
  the Adana Seminary for Girls.

LOS ANGELES CALIFORNIA

HARRY AND HELEN KALPAKIAN
five daughters:
  Angagh Kalpakian 1918—2009 b. Adana, Turkey
    m George Mackellar, three children
  Torkomouhi Kalpakian 1920—1921 b. Adana, Turkey
  Pakradouhi (Peggy) Kalpakian b. 1922 Constantinople
  [author's mother]
    m. William Jess Johnson, four children
  Elizabeth Armenoui Kalpakian 1924—2016 b. Los An-
  geles
    m. Finley Bown, three children

Harriett Meribe Kalpakian 1935—2014 b. Los Angeles
m. Alan Donnell, two children

Margaret Koumjian: 1890—1963 born Makrouli Keishi-
yan [first cousin to Helen Kalpakian] m. Peter Koumjian
(1881—1965) two daughters

Sid Finegold 1918—2016 best friend to Bill Johnson, best
man at his wedding. Became a doctor, married, three children.

IDAHO AND UTAH

JOHNSONS
Gustav Johnson b. Sweden 1840—1896 d. Sacramento,
California
    m. in 1862 Mary (Marna) Anderson (b. in Sweden 1839
    —1930 d. in Idaho)
    two sons, eldest William Andrew Johnson Sr. 1863—
1915
    [Gustav and Mary split up in 1867; in 1868 Mary remar-
ried C. H. Jensen by whom she had many more children.]

Lewis Lance1823—1908 and Temperance Lance 1845—
1913
    seven children of whom,
    Jeannettie Lance 1869—1937 m. William Andrew John-
    son Sr.

William Andrew Johnson Sr. and Jeannettie Lance Johnson
married in 1886

twelve children [one died as a toddler]

William Andrew Johnson Junior 1887–1956 [author's
grandfather]

George 1889–1956

Sydney (Leslie) 1891–1956

Stanley1894–1957

Jess 1896—1978

Anetta 1898–1982

m. William Lutz (d. 1926) m. 2nd Fred Walchli 1884—
1970.

Ila 1900–1903

Lila 1905–1990

m. Laurence Lutz b. c. 1900 died 1988 seven children

Howard 1908–1989 m. two children

Minnie 1911—1999 m. one child

Elaine 1915–1991 Married twice, three children

HENDERSONS

William Ernest Henderson 1872—1947 and Norah Rogers
Henderson 1871—1935

eight children born between 1892 and 1912, including:

Archie b. 1892 d. December 7, 1941

Eva b.1898 d. c.1980 m 1st Charles Bryant in 1915, m.
2nd Ernest L. Farnsworth in 1946

(Evelyn) Mae Henderson (1896–1989) m. William A.
Johnson Jr.

(Mae married twice more, outliving both of these husbands as well.)

WILL JOHNSON AND MAE HENDERSON JOHNSON
six children all but the last born in St. Anthony, Idaho

William Jess Johnson 1918–2012 [author's father]

Evelyn Johnson 1921–1999

Elaine Johnson 1922—2007

Leila Johnson 1924–2004

Frank Johnson 1926–2011

Ronald Johnson 1939 died in infancy

Howard Hale married Jeannettie Johnson's sister Minnie Asola Lance in 1893 and in 1906 became a teacher at Ricks Academy in Rexburg, Idaho.

SAN FERNANDO VALLEY, CALIFORNIA
PEGGY AND BILL JOHNSON parents of

Laura Anne b.1945

Douglas Scott 1950—2021

Helen Kathleen b. 1952

Brian Clark b. 1957

ABOUT THE AUTHOR

Laura Kalpakian is the internationally published author of twenty works of fiction and many short stories. Her most recent novel, *The Great Pretenders* (2019), is a tale of the blacklist era in Hollywood. *Memory Into Memoir: a Handbook for Writers* (nonfiction) appeared in 2021 published by University of New Mexico Press. *American Cookery* was nominated for the 2007 International IMPAC Dublin Literary Award, and she has been awarded an NEA Literature Fellowship and twice the Pacific Northwest Booksellers' Award, as well as a Pen West Award, a Pushcart Prize and the Anahid Award for an American writer of Armenian descent. She has taught fiction, memoir and literature as a visiting writer. Educated on both the east and west coasts, she has a bachelor's and master's degree in history. She can be reached via her website, laurakalpakian.com, Facebook and Twitter.